Abbotsford and Newstead Abbey

Washington Irving

Contents

ABBOTSFORD AND NEWSTEAD ABBEY

BY

Washington Irving

ABBOTSFORD.

By WASHINGTON IRVING.

I sit down to perform my promise of giving you an account of a visit made many years since to Abbotsford. I hope, however, that you do not expect much from me, for the travelling notes taken at the time are so scanty and vague, and my memory so extremely fallacious, that I fear I shall disappoint you with the meagreness and crudeness of my details.

Late in the evening of August 29, 1817, I arrived at the ancient little border town of Selkirk, where I put up for the night. I had come down from Edinburgh, partly to visit Melrose Abbey and its vicinity, but chiefly to get sight of the "mighty minstrel of the north." I had a letter of introduction to him from Thomas Campbell, the poet, and had reason to think, from the interest he had taken in some of my earlier scribblings, that a visit from me would not be deemed an intrusion.

On the following morning, after an early breakfast, I set off in a postchaise for the Abbey. On the way thither I stopped at the gate of Abbotsford, and sent the postilion to the house with the letter of introduction and my card, on which I had written that I was on my way to the ruins of Melrose Abbey, and wished to know whether it would be agreeable to Mr. Scott (he had not yet been made a Baronet) to receive a visit from me in the course of the morning.

While the postilion was on his errand, I had time to survey the
mansion. It stood some short distance below the road, on the side of a
hill sweeping down to the Tweed; and was as yet but a snug gentleman's
cottage, with something rural and picturesque in its appearance. The
whole front was overrun with evergreens, and immediately above the
portal was a great pair of elk horns, branching out from beneath the
foliage, and giving the cottage the look of a hunting lodge. The huge
baronial pile, to which this modest mansion in a manner gave birth was
just emerging into existence; part of the walls, surrounded by
scaffolding, already had risen to the height of the cottage, and the
courtyard in front was encumbered by masses of hewn stone.

The noise of the chaise had disturbed the quiet of the establishment.
Out sallied the warder of the castle, a black greyhound, and, leaping
on one of the blocks of stone, began a furious barking. His alarum
brought out the whole garrison of dogs:

"Both mongrel, puppy, whelp, and hound,
  And curs of low degree;"

all open-mouthed and vociferous.--I should correct my quotation;--not a
cur was to be seen on the premises: Scott was too true a sportsman, and
had too high a veneration for pure blood, to tolerate a mongrel.

In a little while the "lord of the castle" himself made his appearance.
I knew him at once by the descriptions I had read and heard, and the
likenesses that had been published of him. He was tall, and of a large
and powerful frame. His dress was simple, and almost rustic. An old
green shooting-coat, with a dog-whistle at the buttonhole, brown linen
pantaloons, stout shoes that tied at the ankles, and a white hat that
had evidently seen service. He came limping up the gravel walk, aiding
himself by a stout walking-staff, but moving rapidly and with vigor. By

his side jogged along a large iron-gray stag-hound of most grave demeanor, who took no part in the clamor of the canine rabble, but seemed to consider himself bound, for the dignity of the house, to give me a courteous reception.

Before Scott had reached the gate he called out in a hearty tone, welcoming me to Abbotsford, and asking news of Campbell. Arrived at the door of the chaise, he grasped me warmly by the hand: "Come, drive down, drive down to the house," said he, "ye're just in time for breakfast, and afterward ye shall see all the wonders of the Abbey."

I would have excused myself, on the plea of having already made my breakfast. "Hout, man," cried he, "a ride in the morning in the keen air of the Scotch hills is warrant enough for a second breakfast."

I was accordingly whirled to the portal of the cottage, and in a few moments found myself seated at the breakfast-table. There was no one present but the family, which consisted of Mrs. Scott, her eldest daughter Sophia, then a fine girl about seventeen, Miss Ann Scott, two or three years younger, Walter, a well-grown stripling, and Charles, a lively boy, eleven or twelve years of age. I soon felt myself quite at home, and my heart in a glow with the cordial welcome I experienced. I had thought to make a mere morning visit, but found I was not to be let off so lightly. "You must not think our neighborhood is to be read in a morning, like a newspaper," said Scott. "It takes several days of study for an observant traveller that has a relish for auld world trumpery. After breakfast you shall make your visit to Melrose Abbey; I shall not be able to accompany you, as I have some household affairs to attend to, but I will put you in charge of my son Charles, who is very learned in all things touching the old ruin and the neighborhood it stands in, and he and my friend Johnny Bower will tell you the whole truth about it, with a good deal more that you are not called upon to believe-- unless you be a true and nothing-doubting antiquary. When you come back, I'll take you out on a ramble about the neighborhood. To-morrow we will take a look at the Yarrow, and the next day we will drive over to Dryburgh Abbey, which is a fine old ruin well worth your seeing"--in a word, before Scott had got through his plan, I found myself committed for a visit of several days, and it seemed as if a little realm of romance was suddenly opened before me.

          *   *   *   *   *

After breakfast I accordingly set oft for the Abbey with my little friend Charles, whom I found a most sprightly and entertaining companion. He had an ample stock of anecdote about the neighborhood, which he had learned from his father, and many quaint remarks and sly jokes, evidently derived from the same source, all which were uttered with a Scottish accent and a mixture of Scottish phraseology, that gave them additional flavor.

On our way to the Abbey he gave me some anecdotes of Johnny Bower to whom his father had alluded; he was sexton of the parish and custodian of the ruin, employed to keep it in order and show it to strangers;--a worthy little man, not without ambition in his humble sphere. The death of his predecessor had been mentioned in the newspapers, so that his name had appeared in print throughout the land. When Johnny succeeded to the guardianship of the ruin, he stipulated that, on his death, his name should receive like honorable blazon; with this addition, that it should be from, the pen of Scott. The latter gravely pledged himself to pay this tribute to his memory, and Johnny now lived in the proud anticipation of a poetic immortality.

I found Johnny Bower a decent-looking little old man, in blue coat and red waistcoat. He received us with much greeting, and seemed delighted to see my young companion, who was full of merriment and waggery, drawing out his peculiarities for my amusement. The old man was one of

the most authentic and particular of cicerones; he pointed out
everything in the Abbey that had been described by Scott in his "Lay of
the Last Minstrel:" and would repeat, with broad Scottish accent, the
passage which celebrated it.

Thus, in passing through the cloisters, he made me remark the beautiful
carvings of leaves and flowers wrought in stone with the most exquisite
delicacy, and, notwithstanding the lapse of centuries, retaining their
sharpness as if fresh from the chisel; rivalling, as Scott has said,
the real objects of which they were imitations:

  "Nor herb nor flowret glistened there
  But was carved in the cloister arches as fair."

He pointed out, also, among the carved work a nun's head of much
beauty, which he said Scott always stopped to admire--"for the shirra
had a wonderful eye for all sic matters."

I would observe that Scott seemed to derive more consequence in the
neighborhood from being sheriff of the county than from being poet.

In the interior of the Abbey Johnny Bower conducted me to the identical
stone on which Stout "William of Deloraine" and the monk took their seat
on that memorable night when the wizard's book was to be rescued from
the grave. Nay, Johnny had even gone beyond Scott in the minuteness of
his antiquarian research, for he had discovered the very tomb of the
wizard, the position of which had been left in doubt by the poet. This
he boasted to have ascertained by the position of the oriel window, and
the direction in which the moonbeams fell at night, through the stained
glass, casting the shadow to the red cross on the spot; as had all been
specified in the poem. "I pointed out the whole to the shirra," said
he, "and he could na' gainsay but it was varra clear." I found
afterward that Scott used to amuse himself with the simplicity of the

old man, and his zeal in verifying every passage of the poem, as though it had authentic history, and that he always acquiesced in his deductions. I subjoin the description of the wizard's grave, which called forth the antiquarian research of Johnny Bower.

"Lo warrior! now the cross of red,
Points to the grave of the mighty dead;
Slow moved the monk to the broad flag-stone,
Which the bloody cross was traced upon:
He pointed to a sacred nook:
An iron bar the warrior took;
And the monk made a sign with his withered hand,
The grave's huge portal to expand.

"It was by dint of passing strength,
That he moved the massy stone at length.
I would you had been there to see,
How the light broke forth so gloriously,
Streamed upward to the chancel roof,
And through the galleries far aloof!
  And, issuing from the tomb,
Showed the monk's cowl and visage pale,
Danced on the dark brown warrior's mail,
  And kissed his waving plume.

"Before their eyes the wizard lay,
As if he had not been dead a day:
His hoary beard in silver rolled,
He seemed some seventy winters old;
A palmer's amice wrapped him round;
With a wrought Spanish baldrie bound,
  Like a pilgrim from beyond the sea;
His left hand held his book of might;

A silver cross was in his right:
  The lamp was placed beside his knee."

The fictions of Scott had become facts with honest Johnny Bower. From constantly living among the ruins of Melrose Abbey, and pointing out the scenes of the poem, the "Lay of the Last Minstrel" had, in a manner, become interwoven with his whole existence, and I doubt whether he did not now and then mix up his own identity with the personages of some of its cantos.

He could not bear that any other production of the poet should be preferred to the "Lay of the Last Minstrel." "Faith," said he to me, "it's just e'en as gude a thing as Mr. Scott has written--an' if he were stannin' there I'd tell him so--an' then he'd lauff."

He was loud in his praises of the affability of Scott. "He'll come here sometimes," said he, "with great folks in his company, an' the first I know of it is his voice, calling out 'Johnny!--Johnny Bower!'--and when I go out, I am sure to be greeted with a joke or a pleasant word. Hell stand and crack and lauff wi' me, just like an auld wife--and to think that of a man who has such an awfu' knowledge o' history!"

One of the ingenious devices on which the worthy little man prided himself, was to place a visitor opposite to the Abbey, with his back to it, and bid him bend down and look at it between his legs. This, he said, gave an entire different aspect to the ruin. Folks admired the plan amazingly, but as to the "leddies," they were dainty on the matter, and contented themselves with looking from under their arms. As Johnny Bower piqued himself upon showing everything laid down in the poem, there was one passage that perplexed him sadly. It was the opening of one of the cantos:

"If thou would'st view fair Melrose aright,

Go visit it by the pale moonlight:
For the gay beams of lightsome day,
Gild but to flout the ruins gray." etc.

In consequence of this admonition, many of the most devout pilgrims to
the ruin could not be contented with a daylight inspection, and
insisted it could be nothing unless seen by the light of the moon. Now,
unfortunately, the moon shines but for a part of the month; and, what
is still more unfortunate, is very apt in Scotland to be obscured by
clouds and mists. Johnny was sorely puzzled, therefore, how to
accommodate his poetry-struck visitors with this indispensable
moonshine. At length, in a lucky moment, he devised a substitute. This
was a great double tallow candle stuck upon the end of a pole, with
which he could conduct his visitors about the ruins on dark nights, so
much to their satisfaction that, at length, he began to think it even
preferable to the moon itself. "It does na light up a' the Abbey at
since, to be sure," he would say, "but then you can shift it about and
show the auld ruin bit by bit, whiles the moon only shines on one
side."

Honest Johnny Bower! so many years have elapsed since the time I treat
of, that it is more than probable his simple head lies beneath the
walls of his favorite Abbey. It is to be hoped his humble ambition has
been gratified, and his name recorded by the pen of the man he so loved
and honored.

           *   *   *   *   *

After my return from Melrose Abbey, Scott proposed a ramble to show me
something of the surrounding country. As we sallied forth, every dog in
the establishment turned out to attend us. There was the old stag-hound
Maida, that I have already mentioned, a noble animal, and a great
favorite of Scott's, and Hamlet, the black greyhound, a wild,

thoughtless youngster, not yet arrived to the years of discretion; and Finette, a beautiful setter, with soft, silken hair, long pendent ears, and a mild eye, the parlor favorite. When in front of the house, we were joined by a superannuated greyhound, who came from the kitchen wagging his tail, and was cheered by Scott as an old friend and comrade.

In our walks, Scott would frequently pause in conversation to notice his dogs and speak to them, as if rational companions; and indeed there appears to be a vast deal of rationality in these faithful attendants on man, derived from their close intimacy with him. Maida deported himself with a gravity becoming his age and size, and seemed to consider himself called upon to preserve a great degree of dignity and decorum in our society. As he jogged along a little distance ahead of us, the young dogs would gambol about him, leap on his neck, worry at his ears, and endeavor to tease him into a frolic. The old dog would keep on for a long time with imperturbable solemnity, now and then seeming to rebuke the wantonness of his young companions. At length he would make a sudden turn, seize one of them, and tumble him in the dust; then giving a glance at us, as much as to say, "You see, gentlemen, I can't help giving way to this nonsense," would resume his gravity and jog on as before.

Scott amused himself with these peculiarities. "I make no doubt," said he, "when Maida is alone with these young dogs, he throw's gravity aside, and plays the boy as much as any of them; but he is ashamed to do so in our company, and seems to say, 'Ha' done with your nonsense, youngsters: what will the laird and that other gentleman think of me if I give way to such foolery?'"

Maida reminded him, he said, of a scene on board an armed yacht in which he made an excursion with his friend Adam Ferguson. They had taken much notice of the boatswain, who was a fine sturdy seaman, and evidently felt flattered by their attention. On one occasion the crew were "piped to fun," and the sailors were dancing and cutting all kinds of capers to the music of the ship's band. The boatswain looked on with a wistful eye, as if he would like to join in; but a glance at Scott and Ferguson showed that there was a struggle with his dignity, fearing to lessen himself in their eyes. At length one at his messmates came up, and seizing him by the arm, challenged him to a jig. The boatswain, continued Scott, after a little hesitation complied, made an awkward gambol or two, like our friend Maida, but soon gave it up. "It's of no use," said he, jerking up his waistband and giving a side glance at us, "one can't dance always nouther."

Scott amused himself with the peculiarities of another of his dogs, a little shamefaced terrier, with large glassy eyes, one of the most sensitive little bodies to insult and indignity in the world. If ever he whipped him, he said, the little fellow would sneak off and hide himself from the light of day, in a lumber garret, whence there was no drawing him forth but by the sound of the chopping-knife, as if chopping up his victuals, when he would steal forth with humble and downcast look, but would skulk away again if any one regarded him.

While we were discussing the humors and peculiarities of our canine companions, some object provoked their spleen, and produced a sharp and petulant barking from the smaller fry, but it was some time before Maida was sufficiently aroused to ramp forward two or three bounds and join in the chorus, with a deep-mouthed bow-wow!

It was but a transient outbreak, and he returned instantly, wagging his tail, and looking up dubiously in his master's face; uncertain whether he would censure or applaud.

"Aye, aye, old boy!" cried Scott, "you have done wonders. You have shaken the Eildon hills with your roaring; you may now lay by your

artillery for the rest of the day. Maida is like the great gun at
Constantinople," continued he; "it takes so long to get it ready, that
the small guns can fire off a dozen times first, but when it does go
off it plays the very d----l."

These simple anecdotes may serve to show the delightful play of Scott's
humors and feelings in private life. His domestic animals were his
friends; everything about him seemed to rejoice in the light of his
countenance; the face of the humblest dependent brightened at his
approach, as if he anticipated a cordial and cheering word. I had
occasion to observe this particularly in a visit which we paid to a
quarry, whence several men were cutting stone for the new edifice; who
all paused from their labor to have a pleasant "crack wi' the laird."
One of them was a burgess of Selkirk, with whom Scott had some joke
about the old song:

"Up with the Souters o' Selkirk,
  And down with the Earl of Horne."

Another was precentor at the Kirk, and, besides leading the psalmody on
Sunday, taught the lads and lasses of the neighborhood dancing on week
days, in the winter time, when out-of-door labor was scarce.

Among the rest was a tall, straight old fellow, with a healthful
complexion and silver hair, and a small round-crowned white hat. He had
been about to shoulder a nod, but paused, and stood looking at Scott,
with a slight sparkling of his blue eye, as if waiting his turn; for
the old fellow knew himself to be a favorite.

Scott accosted him in an affable tone, and asked for a pinch of snuff.
The old man drew forth a horn snuff-box. "Hoot, man," said Scott, "not
that old mull: where's the bonnie French one that I brought you from
Paris?" "Troth, your honor," replied the old fellow, "sic a mull as

that is nae for week-days."

On leaving the quarry, Scott informed me that when absent at Paris, he had purchased several trifling articles as presents for his dependents, and among others the gay snuff-box in question, which was so carefully reserved for Sundays, by the veteran. "It was not so much the value of the gifts," said he, "that pleased them, as the idea that the laird should think of them when so far away."

The old man in question, I found, was a great favorite with Scott. If I recollect right, he had been a soldier in early life, and his straight, erect person, his ruddy yet rugged countenance, his gray hair, and an arch gleam in his blue eye, reminded me of the description of Edie Ochiltree. I find that the old fellow has since been introduced by Wilkie, in his picture of the Scott family.

    *   *   *   *   *

We rambled on among scenes which had been familiar in Scottish song, and rendered classic by pastoral muse, long before Scott had thrown the rich mantle of his poetry over them. What a thrill of pleasure did I feel when first I saw the broom-covered tops of the Cowden Knowes, peeping above the gray hills of the Tweed: and what touching associations were called up by the sight of Ettrick Vale, Galla Water, and the Braes of Yarrow! Every turn brought to mind some household air --some almost forgotten song of the nursery, by which I had been lulled to sleep in my childhood; and with them the looks and voices of those who had sung them, and who were now no more. It is these melodies, chanted in our ears in the days of infancy, and connected with the memory of those we have loved, and who have passed away, that clothe Scottish landscape with such tender associations. The Scottish songs, in general, have something intrinsically melancholy in them; owing, in all probability, to the pastoral and lonely life of those who composed them: who were often mere shepherds, tending their flocks in the solitary glens, or folding them among the naked hills. Many of these rustic bards have passed away, without leaving a name behind them; nothing remains of them but their sweet and touching songs, which live, like echoes, about the places they once inhabited. Most of these simple effusions of pastoral poets are linked with some favorite haunt of the poet; and in this way, not a mountain or valley, a town or tower, green shaw or running stream, in Scotland, but has some popular air connected with it, that makes its very name a key-note to a whole train of delicious fancies and feelings.

Let me step forward in time, and mention how sensible I was to the power of these simple airs, in a visit which I made to Ayr, the birthplace of Robert Burns. I passed a whole morning about "the banks and braes of bonnie Doon," with his tender little love verses running in my head. I found a poor Scotch carpenter at work among the ruins of Kirk Alloway, which was to be converted into a school-house. Finding the purpose of my visit, he left his work, sat down with me on a grassy grave, close by where Burns' father was buried, and talked of the poet, whom he had known personally. He said his songs were familiar to the poorest and most illiterate of the country folk, "and it seemed to him as if the country had grown more beautiful, since Burns had written his bonnie little songs about it."

I found Scott was quite an enthusiast on the subject of the popular songs of his country, and he seemed gratified to find me so alive to them. Their effect in calling up in my mind the recollections of early times and scenes in which I had first heard them, reminded him, he said, of the lines of his poor Mend, Leyden, to the Scottish muse:

"In youth's first morn, alert and gay,
Ere rolling years had passed away,
  Remembered like a morning dream,

I heard the dulcet measures float,
In many a liquid winding note,
  Along the bank of Teviot's stream.

"Sweet sounds! that oft have soothed to rest
The sorrows of my guileless breast,
  And charmed away mine infant tears;
Fond memory shall your strains repeat,
Like distant echoes, doubly sweet,
  That on the wild the traveller hears."

Scott went on to expatiate on the popular songs of Scotland. "They are
a part of our national inheritance," said he, "and something that we
may truly call our own. They have no foreign taint; they have the pure
breath of the heather and the mountain breeze. All genuine legitimate
races that have descended from the ancient Britons; such as the Scotch,
the Welsh, and the Irish, have national airs. The English have none,
because they are not natives of the soil, or, at least, are mongrels.
Their music is all made up of foreign scraps, like a harlequin jacket,
or a piece of mosaic. Even in Scotland, we have comparatively few
national songs in the eastern part, where we have had most influx of
strangers. A real old Scottish song is a cairngorm--a gem of our own
mountains; or rather, it is a precious relic of old times, that bears
the national character stamped upon it--like a cameo, that shows what
the national visage was in former days, before the breed was crossed."

While Scott was thus discoursing, we were passing up a narrow glen,
with the dogs beating about, to right and left, when suddenly a
blackcock burst upon the wing.

"Aha!" cried Scott, "there will be a good shot for Master Walter; we
must send him this way with his gun, when we go home. Walter's the
family sportsman now, and keeps us in game. I have pretty nigh resigned

my gun to him; for I find I cannot trudge about as briskly as formerly."

Our ramble took us on the hills commanding an extensive prospect. "Now," said Scott, "I have brought you, like the pilgrim in the Pilgrim's Progress, to the top of the Delectable Mountains, that I may show you all the goodly regions hereabouts. Yonder is Lammermuir, and Smalholme; and there you have Gallashiels, and Torwoodlie, and Gallawater; and in that direction you see Teviotdale, and the Braes of Yarrow; and Ettrick stream, winding along, like a silver thread, to throw itself into the Tweed."

He went on thus to call over names celebrated in Scottish song, and most of which had recently received a romantic interest from his own pen. In fact, I saw a great part of the border country spread out before me, and could trace the scenes of those poems and romances which had, in a manner, bewitched the world. I gazed about me for a time with mute surprise, I may almost say with disappointment. I beheld a mere succession of gray waving hills, line beyond line, as far as my eye could reach; monotonous in their aspect, and so destitute of trees, that one could almost see a stout fly walking along their profile; and the far-famed Tweed appeared a naked stream, flowing between bare hills, without a tree or thicket on its banks; and yet, such had been the magic web of poetry and romance thrown over the whole, that it had a greater charm for me than the richest scenery I beheld in England.

I could not help giving utterance to my thoughts. Scott hummed for a moment to himself, and looked grave; he had no idea of having his muse complimented at the expense of his native hills. "It may be partiality," said he, at length; "but to my eye, these gray bills and all this wild border country have beauties peculiar to themselves. I like the very nakedness of the land; it has something bold, and stern, and solitary about it. When I have been for some time in the rich scenery about Edinburgh, which is like ornamented garden land, I begin to wish myself back again among my own honest gray hills; and if I did not see the heather at least once a year, *I think I should die!*"

The last words were said with an honest warmth, accompanied with a thump on the ground with his staff, by way of emphasis, that showed his heart was in his speech. He vindicated the Tweed, too, as a beautiful stream in itself, and observed that he did not dislike it for being bare of trees, probably from having been much of an angler in his time, and an angler does not like to have a stream overhung by trees, which embarrass him in the exercise of his rod and line.

I took occasion to plead, in like manner, the associations of early life, for my disappointment in respect to the surrounding scenery. I had been so accustomed to hills crowned with forests, and streams breaking their way through a wilderness of trees, that all my ideas of romantic landscape were apt to be well wooded.

"Aye, and that's the great charm of your country," cried Scott. "You love the forest as I do the heather--but I would not have you think I do not feel the glory of a great woodland prospect. There is nothing I should like more than to be in the midst of one of your grand, wild, original forests with the idea of hundreds of miles of untrodden forest around me. I once saw, at Leith, an immense stick of timber, just landed from America. It must have been an enormous tree when it stood on its native soil, at its full height, and with all its branches. I gazed at it with admiration; it seemed like one of the gigantic obelisks which are now and then brought from Egypt, to shame the pigmy monuments of Europe; and, in fact, these vast aboriginal trees, that have sheltered the Indians before the intrusion of the white men, are the monuments and antiquities of your country."

The conversation here turned upon Campbell's poem of "Gertrude of

Wyoming," as illustrative of the poetic materials furnished by American scenery. Scott spoke of it in that liberal style in which I always found him to speak of the writings of his contemporaries. He cited several passages of it with great delight. "What a pity it is," said he, "that Campbell does not write more and oftener, and give full sweep to his genius. He has wings that would bear him to the skies; and he does now and then spread them grandly, but folds them up again and resumes his perch, as if he was afraid to launch away. He don't know or won't trust his own strength. Even when he has done a thing well, he has often misgivings about it. He left out several fine passages of his Lochiel, but I got him to restore some of them." Here Scott repeated several passages in a magnificent style. "What a grand idea is that," said he, "about prophetic boding, or, in common parlance, second sight--

'Coming events cast their shadows before.'

"It is a noble thought, and nobly expressed, And there's that glorious little poem, too, of 'Hohenlinden;' after he had written it, he did not seem to think much of it, but considered some of it'd--d drum and trumpet lines.' I got him to recite it to me, and I believe that the delight I felt and expressed had an effect in inducing him to print it. The fact is," added he, "Campbell is, in a manner, a bugbear to himself. The brightness of his early success is a detriment to all his further efforts. He is afraid of the shadow that his own fame casts before him."

While we were thus chatting, we heard the report of a gun among the hills. "That's Walter, I think," said Scott; "he has finished his morning's studies, and is out with his gun. I should not be surprised if he had met with the blackcock; if so, we shall have an addition to our larder, for Walter is a pretty sure shot." I inquired into the nature of Walter's studies. "Faith," said Scott, "I can't say much on that head. I am not over bent upon making prodigies of any of my children. As to Walter, I taught him, while a boy, to ride, and shoot, and speak the truth; as to the other parts of his education, I leave them to a very worthy young man, the son of one of our clergymen, who instructs all my children."

I afterward became acquainted with the young man in question, George Thomson, son of the minister of Melrose, and found him possessed of much learning, intelligence, and modest worth. He used to come every day from his father's residence at Melrose to superintend the studies of the young folks, and occasionally took his meals at Abbotsford, where he was highly esteemed. Nature had cut him out, Scott used to say, for a stalwart soldier, for he was tall, vigorous, active, and fond of athletic exercises, but accident had marred her work, the loss of a limb in boyhood having reduced him to a wooden leg. He was brought up, therefore, for the Church, whence he was occasionally called the Dominie, and is supposed, by his mixture of learning, simplicity, and amiable eccentricity, to have furnished many traits for the character of Dominie Sampson. I believe he often acted as Scott's amanuensis, when composing his novels. With him the young people were occupied in general during the early part of the day, after which they took all kinds of healthful recreations in the open air; for Scott was as solicitous to strengthen their bodies as their minds.

We had not walked much further before we saw the two Miss Scotts advancing along the hillside to meet us. The morning studies being over, they had set off to take a ramble on the hills, and gather heather blossoms, with which to decorate their hair for dinner. As they came bounding lightly like young fawns, and their dresses fluttering in the pure summer breeze, I was reminded of Scott's own description of his children in his introduction to one of the cantos of Marmion--

"My imps, though hardy, bold, and wild,
As best befits the mountain child,

Their summer gambols tell and mourn,
And anxious ask will spring return,
And birds and lambs again be gay,
And blossoms clothe the hawthorn spray?

"Yes, prattlers, yes, the daisy's flower
Again shall paint your summer bower;
Again the hawthorn shall supply
The garlands you delight to tie;
The lambs upon the lea shall bound.
The wild birds carol to the round,
And while you frolic light as they,
Too short shall seem the summer day."

As they approached, the dogs all sprang forward and gambolled around them. They played with them for a time, and then joined us with countenances full of health and glee. Sophia, the eldest, was the most lively and joyous, having much of her father's varied spirit in conversation, and seeming to catch excitement from his words and looks. Ann was of quieter mood, rather silent, owing, in some measure, no doubt, to her being some years younger.

*   *   *   *   *

At dinner Scott had laid by his half-rustic dress, and appeared clad in black. The girls, too, in completing their toilet, had twisted in their hair the sprigs of purple heather which they had gathered on the hillside, and looked all fresh and blooming from their breezy walk.

There was no guest at dinner but myself. Around the table were two or three dogs in attendance. Maida, the old stag-hound, took his seat at Scott's elbow, looking up wistfully in his master's eye, while Finette, the pet spaniel, placed herself near Mrs. Scott, by whom, I soon perceived, she was completely spoiled.

The conversation happening to turn on the merits of his dogs, Scott spoke with great feeling and affection of his favorite, Camp, who is depicted by his side in the earlier engravings of him. He talked of him as of a real friend whom he had lost, and Sophia Scott, looking up archly in his face, observed that Papa shed a few tears when poor Camp died. I may here mention another testimonial of Scott's fondness for his dogs, and his humorous mode of showing it, which I subsequently met with. Rambling with him one morning about the grounds adjacent to the house, I observed a small antique monument, on which was inscribed, in Gothic characters--

"Cy git le preux Percy." (Here lies the brave Percy.)

I paused, supposing it to be the tomb of some stark warrior of the olden time, but Scott drew me on. "Pooh!" cried he, "it's nothing but one of the monuments of my nonsense, of which you'll find enough hereabouts." I learnt afterward that it was the grave of a favorite greyhound. Among the other important and privileged members of the household who figured in attendance at the dinner, was a large gray cat, who, I observed, was regaled from time to time with tit-bits from the table. This sage grimalkin was a favorite of both master and mistress, and slept at night in their room; and Scott laughingly observed, that one of the least wise parts of their establishment was, that the window was left open at night for puss to go in and out. The cat assumed a kind of ascendancy among the quadrupeds--sitting in state in Scott's arm-chair, and occasionally stationing himself on a chair beside the door, as if to review his subjects as they passed, giving each dog a cuff beside the ears as he went by. This clapper-clawing was always taken in good part; it appeared to be, in fact, a mere act of sovereignty on the part of grimalkin, to remind the others of their vassalage; which they acknowledged by the most perfect acquiescence. A general harmony prevailed between sovereign and subjects, and they would all sleep together in the sunshine.

Scott was full of anecdote and conversation during dinner. He made some admirable remarks upon the Scottish character, and spoke strongly in praise of the quiet, orderly, honest conduct of his neighbors, which one would hardly expect, said he, from the descendants of moss troopers, and borderers, in a neighborhood famed in old times for brawl and feud, and violence of all kinds. He said he had, in his official capacity of sheriff, administered the laws for a number of years, during which there had been very few trials. The old feuds and local interests, and rivalries, and animosities of the Scotch, however, still slept, he said, in their ashes, and might easily be roused. Their hereditary feeling for names was still great. It was not always safe to have even the game of foot-ball between villages, the old clannish spirit was too apt to break out. The Scotch, he said, were more revengeful than the English; they carried their resentments longer, and would sometimes lay them by for years, but would be sure to gratify them in the end.

The ancient jealousy between the Highlanders and the Lowlanders still continued to a certain degree, the former looking upon the latter as an inferior race, less brave and hardy, but at the same time, suspecting them of a disposition to take airs upon themselves under the idea of superior refinement. This made them techy and ticklish company for a stranger on his first coming among them; ruffling up and putting themselves upon their mettle on the slightest occasion, so that he had in a manner to quarrel and fight his way into their good graces.

He instanced a case in point in a brother of Mungo Park, who went to take up his residence in a wild neighborhood of the Highlands. He soon found himself considered as an intruder, and that there was a disposition among these cocks of the hills, to fix a quarrel on him, trusting that, being a Lowlander, he would show the white feather.

For a time he bore their flings and taunts with great coolness, until one, presuming on his forbearance, drew forth a dirk, and holding it before him, asked him if he had ever seen a weapon like that in his part of the country. Park, who was a Hercules in frame, seized the dirk, and, with one blow, drove it through an oaken table:--"Yes," replied he, "and tell your friends that a man from the Lowlands drove it where the devil himself cannot draw it out again." All persons were delighted with the feat, and the words that accompanied it. They drank with Park to a better acquaintance, and were staunch friends ever afterwards.

After dinner we adjourned to the drawing-room, which served also for study and library. Against the wall on one side was a long writing-table, with drawers; surmounted by a small cabinet of polished wood, with folding doors richly studded with brass ornaments, within which Scott kept his most valuable papers. Above the cabinet, in a kind of niche, was a complete corslet of glittering steel, with a closed helmet, and flanked by gauntlets and battle-axes. Around were hung trophies and relics of various kinds: a cimeter of Tippoo Saib; a Highland broadsword from Flodden Field; a pair of Rippon spurs from Bannockburn; and above all, a gun which had belonged to Rob Roy, and bore his initials, R.M.G., an object of peculiar interest to me at the time, as it was understood Scott was actually engaged in printing a novel founded on the story of that famous outlaw.

On each side of the cabinet were book-cases, well stored with works of romantic fiction in various languages, many of them rare and antiquated. This, however, was merely his cottage library, the principal part of his books being at Edinburgh.

From this little cabinet of curiosities Scott drew forth a manuscript picked up on the field of Waterloo, containing copies of several songs popular at the time in France. The paper was dabbled with blood--"the very life-blood, very possibly," said Scott, "of some gay young officer, who had cherished these songs as a keepsake from some lady-love in Paris."

He adverted, in a mellow and delightful manner, to the little half-gay, half-melancholy, campaigning song, said to have been composed by General Wolfe, and sung by him at the mess table, on the eve of the storming of Quebec, in which he fell so gloriously:

"Why, soldiers, why,
Should we be melancholy, boys?
Why, soldiers, why,
Whose business 'tis to die!
For should next campaign
Send us to him who made us, boys
We're free from pain:
But should we remain,
A bottle and kind landlady
Makes all well again."

"So," added he, "the poor lad who fell at Waterloo, in all probability, had been singing these songs in his tent the night before the battle, and thinking of the fair dame who had taught him them, and promising himself, should he outlive the campaign, to return to her all glorious from the wars."

I find since that Scott published translations of these songs among some of his smaller poems.

The evening passed away delightfully in this quaint-looking apartment, half study, half drawing-room. Scott read several passages from the old romance of "Arthur," with a fine, deep sonorous voice, and a gravity of tone that seemed to suit the antiquated, black-letter volume. It was a rich treat to hear such a work, read by such a person, and in such a place; and his appearance as he sat reading, in a large armed chair, with his favorite hound Maida at his feet, and surrounded by books and relics, and border trophies, would have formed an admirable and most characteristic picture.

While Scott was reading, the sage grimalkin, already mentioned, had taken his seat in a chair beside the fire, and remained with fixed eye and grave demeanor, as if listening to the reader. I observed to Scott that his cat seemed to have a black-letter taste in literature.

"Ah," said he, "these cats are a very mysterious kind of folk. There is always more passing in their minds than we are aware of. It comes no doubt from their being so familiar with witches and warlocks." He went on to tell a little story about a gude man who was returning to his cottage one night, when, in a lonely out-of-the-way place, he met with a funeral procession of cats all in mourning, bearing one of their race to the grave in a coffin covered with a black velvet pall. The worthy man, astonished and half-frightened at so strange a pageant, hastened home and told what he had seen to his wife and children. Scarce had he finished, when a great black cat that sat beside the fire raised himself up, exclaimed "Then I am king of the cats!" and vanished up the chimney. The funeral seen by the gude man, was one of the cat dynasty.

"Our grimalkin here," added Scott, "sometimes reminds me of the story, by the airs of sovereignty which he assumes; and I am apt to treat him with respect from the idea that he may be a great prince incog., and may some time or other come to the throne."

In this way Scott would make the habits and peculiarities of even the dumb animals about him subjects for humorous remark or whimsical story.

Our evening was enlivened also by an occasional song from Sophia Scott, at the request of her father. She never wanted to be asked twice, but complied frankly and cheerfully. Her songs were all Scotch, sung without any accompaniment, in a simple manner, but with great spirit and expression, and in their native dialects, which gave them an additional charm. It was delightful to hear her carol off in sprightly style, and with an animated air, some of those generous-spirited old Jacobite songs, once current among the adherents of the Pretender in Scotland, in which he is designated by the appellation of "The Young Chevalier."

These songs were much relished by Scott, notwithstanding his loyalty; for the unfortunate "Chevalier" has always been a hero of romance with him, as he has with many other staunch adherents to the House of Hanover, now that the Stuart line has lost all its terrors. In speaking on the subject, Scott mentioned as a curious fact, that, among the papers of the "Chevalier," which had been submitted by government to his inspection, he had found a memorial to Charles from some adherents in America, dated 1778, proposing to set up his standard in the back settlements. I regret that, at the time, I did not make more particular inquiries of Scott on the subject; the document in question, however, in all probability, still exists among the Pretender's papers, which are in the possession of the British Government. In the course of the evening, Scott related the story of a whimsical picture hanging in the room, which had been drawn for him by a lady of his acquaintance. It represented the doleful perplexity of a wealthy and handsome young English knight of the olden time, who, in the course of a border foray, had been captured and carried off to the castle of a hard-headed and high-handed old baron. The unfortunate youth was thrown into a dungeon, and a tall gallows erected before the castle gate for his execution. When all was ready, he was brought into the castle hall where the grim baron was seated in state, with his warriors armed to the teeth around him, and was given his choice, either to swing on the gibbet or to marry the baron's daughter. The last may be thought an easy alternative, but unfortunately, the baron's young lady was hideously ugly, with a mouth from ear to ear, so that not a suitor was to be had for her, either for love or money, and she was known throughout the border country by the name of Muckle-mouthed Mag!

The picture in question represented the unhappy dilemma of the handsome youth. Before him sat the grim baron, with a face worthy of the father of such a daughter, and looking daggers and ratsbane. On one side of him was Muckle-mouthed Mag, with an amorous smile across the whole breadth of her countenance, and a leer enough to turn a man to stone; on the other side was the father confessor, a sleek friar, jogging the youth's elbow, and pointing to the gallows, seen in perspective through the open portal.

The story goes, that after long laboring in mind, between the altar and the halter, the love of life prevailed, and the youth resigned himself to the charms of Muckle-mouthed Mag. Contrary to all the probabilities of romance, the match proved a happy one. The baron's daughter, if not beautiful, was a most exemplary wife; her husband was never troubled with any of those doubts and jealousies which sometimes mar the happiness of connubial life, and was made the father of a fair and undoubtedly legitimate hue, which still flourishes on the border.

I give but a faint outline of the story from vague recollection; it may, perchance, be more richly related elsewhere, by some one who may retain something of the delightful humor with which Scott recounted it.

When I retired for the night, I found it almost impossible to sleep; the idea of being under the roof of Scott; of being on the borders of the Tweed, in the very centre of that region which had for some time past been the favorite scene of romantic fiction; and above all, the recollections of the ramble I had taken, the company in which I had taken it, and the conversation which had passed, all fermented in my mind, and nearly drove sleep from my pillow.

*   *   *   *   *

On the following morning, the sun darted his beams from over the hills through the low lattice window. I rose at an early hour, and looked out between the branches of eglantine which overhung the casement. To my surprise Scott was already up and forth, seated on a fragment of stone, and chatting with the workmen employed on the new building. I had supposed, after the time he had wasted upon me yesterday, he would be closely occupied this morning, but he appeared like a man of leisure, who had nothing to do but bask in the sunshine and amuse himself.

I soon dressed myself and joined him. He talked about his proposed plans of Abbotsford; happy would it have been for him could he have contented himself with his delightful little vine-covered cottage, and the simple, yet hearty and hospitable style, in which he lived at the time of my visit. The great pile of Abbotsford, with the huge expense it entailed upon him, of servants, retainers, guests, and baronial style, was a drain upon his purse, a tax upon his exertions, and a weight upon his mind, that finally crushed him.

As yet, however, all was in embryo and perspective, and Scott pleased himself with picturing out his future residence, as he would one of the fanciful creations of his own romances. "It was one of his air castles," he said, "which he was reducing to solid stone and mortar." About the place were strewed various morsels from the ruins of Melrose Abbey, which were to be incorporated in his mansion. He had already constructed out of similar materials a kind of Gothic shrine over a spring, and had surmounted it by a small stone cross.

Among the relics from the Abbey which lay scattered before us, was a most quaint and antique little lion, either of red stone, or painted red, which hit my fancy. I forgot whose cognizance it was; but I shall never forget the delightful observations concerning old Melrose to which it accidentally gave rise. The Abbey was evidently a pile that called up all Scott's poetic and romantic feelings; and one to which he was enthusiastically attached by the most fanciful and delightful of his early associations. He spoke of it, I may say, with affection. "There is no telling," said he, "what treasures are hid in that glorious old pile. It is a famous place for antiquarian plunder; there are such rich bits of old time sculpture for the architect, and old time story for the poet. There is as rare picking in it as a Stilton cheese, and in the same taste--the mouldier the better."

He went on to mention circumstances of "mighty import" connected with the Abbey, which had never been touched, and which had even escaped the researches of Johnny Bower. The heart of Robert Bruce, the hero of Scotland, had been buried in it. He dwelt on the beautiful story of Bruce's pious and chivalrous request in his dying hour, that his heart might be carried to the Holy Land and placed in the Holy Sepulchre, in fulfilment of a vow of pilgrimage; and of the loyal expedition of Sir James Douglas to convey the glorious relic. Much might be made, he said, out of the adventures of Sir James in that adventurous age; of his fortunes in Spain, and his death in a crusade against the Moors; with the subsequent fortunes of the heart of Robert Bruce, until it was brought back to its native land, and enshrined within the holy walls of old Melrose.

As Scott sat on a stone talking in this way, and knocking with his staff against the little red lion which lay prostrate before him, his gray eyes twinkled beneath his shagged eyebrows; scenes, images, incidents, kept breaking upon his mind as he proceeded, mingled with touches of the mysterious and supernatural as connected with the heart of Bruce. It seemed as if a poem or romance were breaking vaguely on his imagination. That he subsequently contemplated something of the kind, as connected with this subject, and with his favorite ruin of Melrose, is evident from his introduction to "The Monastery;" and it is a pity that he never succeeded in following out these shadowy, but enthusiastic conceptions.

A summons to breakfast broke off our conversation, when I begged to recommend to Scott's attention my friend the little red lion, who had led to such an interesting topic, and hoped he might receive some niche or station in the future castle, worthy of his evident antiquity and apparent dignity. Scott assured me, with comic gravity, that the valiant little lion should be most honorably entertained; I hope, therefore, that he still flourishes at Abbotsford.

Before dismissing the theme of the relics from the Abbey, I will mention another, illustrative of Scott's varied humors. This was a human skull, which had probably belonged of yore to one of those jovial friars, so honorably mentioned in the old border ballad:

"O the monks of Melrose made gude kale
On Fridays, when they fasted;
They wanted neither beef nor ale,
As long as their neighbors lasted."

This skull he had caused to be cleaned and varnished, and placed it on a chest of drawers in his chamber, immediately opposite his bed; where I have seen it, grinning most dismally. It was an object of great awe and horror to the superstitious housemaids; and Scott used to amuse himself with their apprehensions. Sometimes, in changing his dress, he would leave his neck-cloth coiled round it like a turban, and none of the "lasses" dared to remove it. It was a matter of great wonder and speculation among them that the laird should have such an "awsome fancy for an auld girning skull."

At breakfast that morning Scott gave an amusing account of a little
Highlander called Campbell of the North, who had a lawsuit of many
years' standing with a nobleman in his neighborhood about the
boundaries of their estates. It was the leading object of the little
man's life; the running theme of all his conversations; he used to
detail all the circumstances at full length to everybody he met, and,
to aid him in his description of the premises, and make his story "mair
preceese," he had a great map made of his estate, a huge roll several
feet long, which he used to carry about on his shoulder. Campbell was a
long-bodied, but short and bandy-legged little man, always clad in the
Highland garb; and as he went about with this great roll on his
shoulder, and his little legs curving like a pair of parentheses below
his kilt, he was an odd figure to behold. He was like little David
shouldering the spear of Goliath, which was "like unto a weaver's
beam."

Whenever sheep-shearing was over, Campbell used to set out for
Edinburgh to attend to his lawsuit. At the inns he paid double for all
his meals and his night's lodgings, telling the landlords to keep it in
mind until his return, so that he might come back that way at free
cost; for he knew, he said, that he would spend all his money among the
lawyers at Edinburgh, so he thought it best to secure a retreat home
again.

On one of his visits he called upon his lawyer, but was told he was not
at home, but his lady was. "It's just the same thing," said little
Campbell. On being shown into the parlor, he unrolled his map, stated
his case at full length, and, having gone through with his story, gave
her the customary fee. She would have declined it, but he insisted on
her taking it. "I ha' had just as much pleasure," said he, "in telling
the whole tale to you, as I should have had in telling it to your

husband, and I believe full as much profit."

The last time he saw Scott, he told him he believed he and the laird were near a settlement, as they agreed to within a few miles of the boundary. If I recollect right, Scott added that he advised the little man to consign his cause and his map to the care of "Slow Willie Mowbray," of tedious memory, an Edinburgh worthy, much employed by the country people, for he tired out everybody in office by repeated visits and drawling, endless prolixity, and gained every suit by dint of boring.

These little stories and anecdotes, which abounded in Scott's conversation, rose naturally out of the subject, arid were perfectly unforced; though, in thus relating them in a detached way, without the observations or circumstances which led to them, and which have passed from my recollection, they want their setting to give them proper relief. They will serve, however, to show the natural play of his mind, in its familiar moods, and its fecundity in graphic and characteristic detail.

His daughter Sophia and his son Charles were those of his family who seemed most to feel and understand his humors, and to take delight in his conversation. Mrs. Scott did not always pay the same attention, and would now and then make a casual remark which would operate a little like a damper. Thus, one morning at breakfast, when Dominie Thomson, the tutor, was present, Scott was going on with great glee to relate an anecdote of the laird of Macnab, "who, poor fellow," premised he, "is dead and gone--" "Why, Mr. Scott," exclaimed the good lady, "Macnab's not dead, is he?" "Faith, my dear," replied Scott, with humorous gravity, "if he's not dead they've done him great injustice--for they've buried him."

The joke passed harmless and unnoticed by Mrs. Scott, but hit the poor

Dominie just as he had raised a cup of tea to his lips, causing a burst of laughter which sent half of the contents about the table. After breakfast, Scott was occupied for some time correcting proof-sheets which he had received by the mail. The novel of Rob Roy, as I have already observed, was at that time in the press, and I supposed them to be the proof-sheets of that work. The authorship of the Waverley novels was still a matter of conjecture and uncertainty; though few doubted their being principally written by Scott. One proof to me of his being the author, was that he never adverted to them. A man so fond of anything Scottish, and anything relating to national history or local legend, could not have been mute respecting such productions, had they been written by another. He was fond of quoting the works of his contemporaries; he was continually reciting scraps of border songs, or relating anecdotes of border story. With respect to his own poems, and their merits, however, he was mute, and while with him I observed a scrupulous silence on the subject.

I may here mention a singular fact, of which I was not aware at the time, that Scott was very reserved with his children respecting his own writings, and was even disinclined to their reading his romantic poems. I learnt this, some time after, from a passage in one of his letters to me, adverting to a set of the American miniature edition of his poems, which, on my return to England, I forwarded to one of the young ladies. "In my hurry," writes he, "I have not thanked you, in Sophia's name, for the kind attention which furnished her with the American volumes. I am not quite sure I can add my own, since you have made her acquainted with much more of papa's folly than she would otherwise have learned; for I have taken special care they should never see any of these things during their earlier years."

To return to the thread of my narrative. When Scott had got through his brief literary occupation, we set out on a ramble. The young ladies started to accompany us, but they had not gone far, when they met a poor old laborer and his distressed family, and turned back to take them to the house, and relieve them.

On passing the bounds of Abbotsford, we came upon a bleak-looking farm, with a forlorn, crazy old manse, or farmhouse, standing in naked desolation. This, however, Scott told me, was an ancient hereditary property called Lauckend, about as valuable as the patrimonial estate of Don Quixote, and which, in like manner, conferred an hereditary dignity upon its proprietor, who was a laird, and, though poor as a rat, prided himself upon his ancient blood, and the standing of his house. He was accordingly called Lauckend, according to the Scottish custom of naming a man after his family estate, but he was more generally known through the country round by the name of Lauckie Long Legs, from the length of his limbs. While Scott was giving this account of him, we saw him at a distance striding along one of his fields, with his plaid fluttering about him, and he seemed well to deserve his appellation, for he looked all legs and tartan.

Lauckie knew nothing of the world beyond his neighborhood. Scott told me that on returning to Abbotsford from his visit to France, immediately after the war, he was called on by his neighbors generally to inquire after foreign parts. Among the number came Lauckie Long Legs and an old brother as ignorant as himself. They had many inquiries to make about the French, whom they seemed to consider some remote and semi-barbarous horde--"And what like are thae barbarians in their own country?" said Lauckie, "can they write?--can they cipher?" He was quite astonished to learn that they were nearly as much advanced in civilization as the gude folks of Abbotsford.

After living for a long time in single blessedness, Lauckie all at once, and not long before my visit to the neighborhood, took it into his head to get married. The neighbors were all surprised; but the family connection, who were as proud as they were poor, were grievously scandalized, for they thought the young woman on whom he had set his mind quite beneath him. It was in vain, however, that they remonstrated on the misalliance he was about to make; he was not to be swayed from his determination. Arraying himself in his best, and saddling a gaunt steed that might have rivalled Rosinante, and placing a pillion behind his saddle, he departed to wed and bring home the humble lassie who was to be made mistress of the venerable hovel of Lauckend, and who lived in a village on the opposite side of the Tweed.

A small event of the kind makes a great stir in a little quiet country neighborhood. The word soon circulated through the village of Melrose, and the cottages in its vicinity, that Lauckie Long Legs had gone over the Tweed to fetch home his bride. All the good folks assembled at the bridge to await his return. Lauckie, however, disappointed them; for he crossed the river at a distant ford, and conveyed his bride safe to his mansion without being perceived. Let me step forward in the course of events, and relate the fate of poor Lauckie, as it was communicated to me a year or two afterward in letter by Scott. From the time of his marriage he had no longer any peace, owing to the constant intermeddling of his relations, who would not permit him to be happy in his own way, but endeavored to set him at variance with his wife. Lauckie refused to credit any of their stories to her disadvantage; but the incessant warfare he had to wage in defence of her good name, wore out both flesh and spirit. His last conflict was with his own brothers, in front of his paternal mansion. A furious scolding match took place between them; Lauckie made a vehement profession of faith in favor of her immaculate honesty, and then fell dead at the threshold of his own door. His person, his character, his name, his story, and his fate, entitled him to be immortalized in one of Scott's novels, and I looked to recognize him in some of the succeeding works from his pen; but I looked in vain.

*   *   *   *   *

After passing by the domains of honest Lauckie, Scott pointed out, at a distance, the Eildon stone. There in ancient days stood the Eildon tree, beneath which Thomas the Rhymer, according to popular tradition, dealt forth his prophecies, some of which still exist in antiquated ballads.

Here we turned up a little glen with a small burn or brook whimpering and dashing along it, making an occasional waterfall, and overhung in some places with mountain ash and weeping birch. We are now, said Scott, treading classic, or rather fairy ground. This is the haunted glen of Thomas the Rhymer, where he met with the queen of fairy land, and this the bogle burn, or goblin brook, along which she rode on her dapple-gray palfrey, with silver bells ringing at the bridle.

"Here," said he, pausing, "is Huntley Bank, on which Thomas the Rhymer lay musing and sleeping when he saw, or dreamt he saw, the queen of Elfland:

"'True Thomas lay on Huntlie bank;
A ferlie he spied wi' his e'e;
And there he saw a ladye bright,
Come riding down by the Eildon tree.

"'Her skirt was o' the grass-green silk,
Her mantle o' the velvet fyne;
At ilka tett of her horse's mane
Hung fifty siller bells and nine.'"

Here Scott repeated several of the stanzas and recounted the
circumstance of Thomas the Rhymer's interview with the fairy, and his
being transported by her to fairy land--

"And til seven years were gone and past,
  True Thomas on earth was never seen."

"It's a fine old story," said he, "and might be wrought up into a
capital tale."

Scott continued on, leading the way as usual, and limping up the wizard
glen, talking as he went, but, as his back was toward me, I could only
hear the deep growling tones of his voice, like the low breathing of an
organ, without distinguishing the words, until pausing, and turning his
face toward me, I found he was reciting some scrap of border minstrelsy
about Thomas the Rhymer. This was continually the case in my ramblings
with him about this storied neighborhood. His mind was fraught with the
traditionary fictions connected with every object around him, and he
would breathe it forth as he went, apparently as much for his own
gratification as for that of his companion.

"Nor hill, nor brook, we paced along,

But had its legend or its song."

His voice was deep and sonorous, he spoke with a Scottish accent, and
with somewhat of the Northumbrian "burr," which, to my mind, gave a
Doric strength and simplicity to his elocution. His recitation of
poetry was, at times, magnificent.

I think it was in the course of this ramble that my friend Hamlet, the
black greyhound, got into a bad scrape. The dogs were beating about the
glens and fields as usual, and had been for some time out of sight,

when we heard a barking at some distance to the left. Shortly after we saw some sheep scampering on the hills, with the dogs after them. Scott applied to his lips the ivory whistle, always hanging at his button-hole, and soon called in the culprits, excepting Hamlet. Hastening up a bank which commanded a view along a fold or hollow of the hills, we beheld the sable prince of Denmark standing by the bleeding body of a sheep. The carcass was still warm, the throat bore marks of the fatal grip, and Hamlet's muzzle was stained with blood. Never was culprit more completely caught in *flagrante delicto*. I supposed the doom of poor Hamlet to be sealed; for no higher offence can be committed by a dog in a country abounding with sheep-walks. Scott, however, had a greater value for his dogs than for his sheep. They were his companions and friends. Hamlet, too, though an irregular, impertinent kind of youngster, was evidently a favorite. He would not for some time believe it could be he who had killed the sheep. It must have been some cur of the neighborhood, that had made off on our approach and left poor Hamlet in the lurch. Proofs, however, were too strong, and Hamlet was generally condemned. "Well, well," said Scott, "it's partly my own fault. I have given up coursing for some time past, and the poor dog has had no chance after game to take the fire edge off of him If he was put after a hare occasionally he never would meddle with sheep."

I understood, afterward, that Scott actually got a pony, and went out now and then coursing with Hamlet, who, in consequence, showed no further inclination for mutton.

*   *   *   *   *

A further stroll among the hills brought us to what Scott pronounced the remains of a Roman camp, and as we sat upon a hillock which had once formed a part of the ramparts, he pointed out the traces of the lines and bulwarks, and the pratorium, and showed a knowledge of castramatation that would not have disgraced the antiquarian Oldbuck himself. Indeed, various circumstances that I observed about Scott during my visit, concurred to persuade me that many of the antiquarian humors of Monkbarns were taken from his own richly compounded character, and that some of the scenes and personages of that admirable novel were furnished by his immediate neighborhood.

He gave me several anecdotes of a noted pauper named Andrew Gemmells, or Gammel, as it was pronounced, who had once flourished on the banks of Galla Water, immediately opposite Abbotsford, and whom he had seen and talked and joked with when a boy; and I instantly recognized the likeness of that mirror of philosophic vagabonds and Nestor of beggars, Edie Ochiltree. I was on the point of pronouncing the name and recognizing the portrait, when I recollected the incognito observed by Scott with respect to his novels, and checked myself; but it was one among many things that tended to convince me of his authorship.

His picture of Andrew Gemmells exactly accorded with that of Edie as to his height, carriage, and soldier-like air, as well as his arch and sarcastic humor. His home, if home he had, was at Galashiels; but he went "daundering" about the country, along the green shaws and beside the burns, and was a kind of walking chronicle throughout the valleys of the Tweed, the Ettrick, and the Yarrow; carrying the gossip from house to house, commenting on the inhabitants and their concerns, and never hesitating to give them a dry rub as to any of their faults or follies.

A shrewd beggar like Andrew Gemmells, Scott added, who could sing the old Scotch airs, tell stories and traditions, and gossip away the long winter evenings, was by no means an unwelcome visitor at a lonely manse or cottage. The children would run to welcome him, and place his stool in a warm corner of the ingle nook, and the old folks would receive him as a privileged guest.

As to Andrew, he looked upon them all as a parson does upon his parishioners, and considered the alms he received as much his due as the other does his tithes. "I rather think," added Scott, "Andrew considered himself more of a gentleman than those who toiled for a living, and that he secretly looked down upon the painstaking peasants that fed and sheltered him."

He had derived his aristocratical notions in some degree from being admitted occasionally to a precarious sociability with some of the small country gentry, who were sometimes in want of company to help while away the time. With these Andrew would now and then play at cards and dice, and he never lacked "siller in pouch" to stake on a game, which he did with a perfect air of a man to whom money was a matter of little moment, and no one could lose his money with more gentlemanlike coolness.

Among those who occasionally admitted him to this familiarity, was old John Scott of Galla, a man of family, who inhabited his paternal mansion of Torwoodlee. Some distinction of rank, however, was still kept up. The laird sat on the inside of the window and the beggar on the outside, and they played cards on the sill.

Andrew now and then told the laird a piece of his mind very freely; especially on one occasion, when he had sold some of his paternal lands to build himself a larger house with the proceeds. The speech of honest Andrew smacks of the shrewdness of Edie Ochiltree.

"It's a' varra weel--it's a' varra weel, Torwoodlee," said he; "but who would ha' thought that your father's son would ha' sold two gude estates to build a shaw's (cuckoo's) nest on the side of a hill?"

*   *   *   *   *

That day there was an arrival at Abbotsford of two English tourists; one a gentleman of fortune and landed estate, the other a young clergyman whom he appeared to have under his patronage, and to have brought with him as a travelling companion.

The patron was one of those well-bred, commonplace gentlemen with which England is overrun. He had great deference for Scott, and endeavored to acquit himself learnedly in his company, aiming continually at abstract disquisitions, for which Scott had little relish. The conversation of the latter, as usual, was studded with anecdotes and stories, some of them of great pith and humor; the well-bred gentleman was either too dull to feel their point, or too decorous to indulge in hearty merriment; the honest parson, on the contrary, who was not too refined to be happy, laughed loud and long at every joke, and enjoyed them with the zest of a man who has more merriment in his heart than coin in his pocket.

After they were gone, some comments were made upon their different deportments. Scott spoke very respectfully of the good breeding and measured manners of the man of wealth, but with a kindlier feeling of the honest parson, and the homely but hearty enjoyment with which he relished every pleasantry. "I doubt," said he, "whether the parson's lot in life is not the best; if he cannot command as many of the good things of this world by his own purse as his patron can, he beats him all hollow in his enjoyment of them when set before him by others. Upon the whole," added he, "I rather think I prefer the honest parson's good humor to his patron's good breeding; I have a great regard for a hearty laugher."

He went on to speak of the great influx of English travellers which of late years had inundated Scotland; and doubted whether they had not injured the old-fashioned Scottish character. "Formerly they came here occasionally as sportsmen," said he, "to shoot moor game, without any idea of looking at scenery; and they moved about the country in hardy simple style, coping with the country people in their own way; but now they come rolling about in their equipages, to see ruins, and spend money, and their lavish extravagance has played the vengeance with the common people. It has made them rapacious in their dealings with strangers, greedy after money, and extortionate in their demands for the most trivial services. Formerly," continued he, "the poorer classes of our people were, comparatively, disinterested; they offered their services gratuitously, in promoting the amusement, or aiding the curiosity of strangers, and were gratified by the smallest compensation; but now they make a trade of showing rocks and ruins, and are as greedy as Italian cicerones. They look upon the English as so many walking money-bags; the more they are shaken and poked, the more they will leave behind them."

I told him that he had a great deal to answer for on that head, since it was the romantic associations he had thrown by his writings over so many out-of-the-way places in Scotland, that had brought in the influx of curious travellers.

Scott laughed, and said he believed I might be in some measure in the right, as he recollected a circumstance in point. Being one time at Glenross, an old woman who kept a small inn, which had but little custom, was uncommonly officious in her attendance upon him, and absolutely incommoded him with her civilities. The secret at length came out. As he was about to depart, she addressed him with many curtsies, and said she understood he was the gentleman that had written a bonnie book about Loch Katrine. She begged him to write a little about their lake also, for she understood his book had done the inn at Loch Katrine a muckle deal of good.

On the following day I made an excursion with Scott and the young
ladies to Dryburgh Abbey. We went in an open carriage, drawn by two
sleek old black horses, for which Scott seemed to have an affection, as
he had for every dumb animal that belonged to him. Our road lay through
a variety of scenes, rich in poetical and historical associations,
about most of which Scott had something to relate. In one part of the
drive, he pointed to an old border keep, or fortress, on the summit of
a naked hill, several miles off, which he called Smallholm Tower, and a
rocky knoll on which it stood, the "Sandy Knowe crags." It was a place,
he said, peculiarly dear to him, from the recollections of childhood.
His father had lived there in the old Smallholm Grange, or farm-house;
and he had been sent there, when but two years old, on account of his
lameness, that he might have the benefit of the pure air of the hills,
and be under the care of his grandmother and aunts. In the introduction
of one of the cantos of Marmion, he has depicted his grandfather, and
the fireside of the farm-house; and has given an amusing picture of
himself in his boyish years:

> "Still with vain fondness could I trace
> Anew each kind familiar face,
> That brightened at our evening fire;
> From the thatched mansion's gray-haired sire,
> Wise without learning plain and good,
> And sprung of Scotland's gentler blood;
> Whose eye in age, quick, clear and keen.
> Showed what in youth its glance had been;
> Whose doom discording neighbors sought,
> Content with equity unbought;
> To him the venerable priest,
> Our frequent and familiar guest,
> Whose life and manners well could paint
> Alike the student and the saint;

Alas! whose speech too oft I broke
With gambol rude and timeless joke;
For I was wayward, bold, and wild,
A self-willed imp, a grandame's child;
But half a plague, and half a jest,
Was still endured, beloved, carest."

It was, he said, during his residence at Smallholm crags that he first imbibed his passion for legendary tales, border traditions, and old national songs and ballads. His grandmother and aunts were well versed in that kind of lore, so current in Scottish country life. They used to recount them in long, gloomy winter days, and about the ingle nook at night, in conclave with their gossip visitors; and little Walter would sit and listen with greedy ear; thus taking into his infant mind the seeds of many a splendid fiction.

There was an old shepherd, he said, in the service of the family, who used to sit under the sunny wall, and tell marvellous stories, and recite old time ballads, as he knitted stockings. Scott used to be wheeled out in his chair, in fine weather, and would sit beside the old man, and listen to him for hours.

The situation of Sandy Knowe was favorable both for storyteller and listener. It commanded a wide view over all the border country, with its feudal towers, its haunted glens, and wizard streams. As the old shepherd told his tales, he could point out the very scene of action. Thus, before Scott could walk, he was made familiar with the scenes of his future stories; they were all seen as through a magic medium, and took that tinge of romance, which they ever after retained in his imagination. From the height of Sandy Knowe, he may be said to have had the first look-out upon the promised land of his future glory.

On referring to Scott's works, I find many of the circumstances related in this conversation, about the old tower, and the boyish scenes connected with it, recorded in the introduction to Marmion, already cited. This was frequently the case with Scott; incidents and feelings that had appeared in his writings, were apt to be mingled up in his conversation, for they had been taken from what he had witnessed and felt in real life, and were connected with those scenes among which he lived, and moved, and had his being. I make no scruple at quoting the passage relative to the tower, though it repeats much of the foregone imagery, and with vastly superior effect:

Thus, while I ape the measure wild
Of tales that charmed me yet a child,
Rude though they be, still with the chime
Return the thoughts of early time;
And feelings roused in life's first day,
Glow in the line, and prompt the lay.
Then rise those crags, that mountain tower.
Which charmed my fancy's wakening hour,
Though no broad river swept along
To claim perchance heroic song;
Though sighed no groves in summer gale
To prompt of love a softer tale;
Though scarce a puny streamlet's speed
Claimed homage from a shepherd's reed;
Yet was poetic impulse given,
By the green hill and clear blue heaven.
It was a barren scene, and wild,
Where naked cliffs were rudely piled;
But ever and anon between
Lay velvet tufts of loveliest green;
And well the lonely infant knew
Recesses where the wall-flower grew,
And honey-suckle loved to crawl

Up the low crag and ruined wall.
I deemed such nooks the sweetest shade
The sun in all his round surveyed;
And still I thought that shattered tower
The mightiest work of human power;
And marvell'd as the aged hind
With some strange tale bewitched my mind,
Of forayers, who, with headlong force,
Down from that strength had spurred their horse,
Their southern rapine to renew,
Far in the distant Cheviot's blue,
And, home returning, filled the hall
With revel, wassail-rout, and brawl--
Methought that still, with tramp and clang
The gate-way's broken arches rang;
Methought grim features, seamed with scars,
Glared through the window's rusty bars.
And ever by the winter hearth,
Old tales I heard of woe or mirth,
Of lovers' slights, of ladies' charms,
Of witches' spells, of warriors' arms;
Of patriot battles, won of old,
By Wallace wight and Bruce the bold;
Of later fields of feud and fight,
When pouring from the Highland height,
The Scottish clans, in headlong sway,
Had swept the scarlet ranks away.
While stretched at length upon the floor,
Again I fought each combat o'er.
Pebbles and shells, in order laid,
The mimic ranks of war displayed;
And onward still the Scottish Lion bore,
And still the scattered Southron fled before."

Scott eyed the distant height of Sandy Knowe with an earnest gaze as we rode along, and said he had often thought of buying the place, repairing the old tower, and making it his residence. He has in some measure, however, paid off his early debt of gratitude, in clothing it with poetic and romantic associations, by his tale of "The Eve of St. John." It is to be hoped that those who actually possess so interesting a monument of Scott's early days, will preserve it from further dilapidation.

Not far from Sandy Knowe, Scott pointed out another old border hold, standing on the summit of a hill, which had been a kind of enchanted castle to him in his boyhood. It was the tower of Bemerside, the baronial residence of the Haigs, or De Hagas, one of the oldest families of the border. "There had seemed to him," he said, "almost a wizard spell hanging over it, in consequence of a prophecy of Thomas the Rhymer, in which, in his young days, he most potently believed:"

"Betide, betide, whate'er betide,
  Haig shall be Haig of Bemerside."

Scott added some particulars which showed that, in the present instance, the venerable Thomas had not proved a false prophet, for it was a noted fact that, amid all the changes and chances of the border; through all the feuds, and forays, and sackings, and burnings, which had reduced most of the castles to ruins, and the proud families that once possessed them to poverty, the tower of Bemerside still remained unscathed, and was still the stronghold of the ancient family of Haig.

Prophecies, however, often insure their own fulfilment. It is very probable that the prediction of Thomas the Rhymer has linked the Haigs to their tower, as their rock of safety, and has induced them to cling to it almost superstitiously, through hardships and inconveniences that would, otherwise, have caused its abandonment.

I afterwards saw, at Dryburgh Abbey, the burying place of this predestinated and tenacious family, the inscription of which showed the value they set upon their antiquity:

Locus Sepultura, Antiquessima Familia De Haga De Bemerside.

In reverting to the days of his childhood, Scott observed that the lameness which had disabled him in infancy gradually decreased; he soon acquired strength in his limbs, and though he always limped, he became, even in boyhood, a great walker. He used frequently to stroll from home and wander about the country for days together, picking up all kinds of local gossip, and observing popular scenes and characters. His father used to be vexed with him for this wandering propensity, and, shaking his head, would say he fancied the boy would make nothing but a peddler. As he grew older he became a keen sportsman, and passed much of his time hunting and shooting. His field sports led him into the most wild and unfrequented parts of the country, and in this way he picked up much of that local knowledge which he has since evinced in his writings.

His first visit to Loch Katrine, he says, was in his boyish days, on a shooting excursion. The island, which he has made the romantic residence of the "Lady of the Lake," was then garrisoned by an old man and his wife. Their house was vacant; they had put the key under the door, and were absent fishing. It was at that time a peaceful residence, but became afterward a resort of smugglers, until they were ferreted out.

In after years, when Scott began to turn this local knowledge to literary account, he revisited many of those scenes of his early ramblings, and endeavored to secure the fugitive remains of the traditions and songs that had charmed his boyhood. When collecting materials for his "Border Minstrelsy," he used, he said, to go from cottage to cottage, and make the old wives repeat all they knew, if but two lines; and by putting these scraps together, he retrieved many a fine characteristic old ballad or tradition from oblivion.

I regret to say that I can scarce recollect anything of our visit to Dryburgh Abbey. It is on the estate of the Earl of Buchan. The religious edifice is a mere ruin, rich in Gothic antiquities, but especially interesting to Scott, from containing the family vault, and the tombs and monuments of his ancestors. He appeared to feel much chagrin at their being in the possession, and subject to the intermeddlings of the Earl, who was represented as a nobleman of an eccentric character. The latter, however, set great value on these sepulchral relics, and had expressed a lively anticipation of one day or other having the honor of burying Scott, and adding his monument to the collection, which he intended should be worthy of the "mighty minstrel of the north"--a prospective compliment which was by no means relished by the object of it. One of my pleasant rambles with Scott, about the neighborhood of Abbotsford, was taken in company with Mr. William Laidlaw, the steward of his estate. This was a gentleman for whom Scott entertained a particular value. He had been born to a competency, had been well educated, his mind was richly stored with varied information, and he was a man of sterling moral worth. Having been reduced by misfortune, Scott had got him to take charge of his estate. He lived at a small farm on the hillside above Abbotsford, and was treated by Scott as a cherished and confidential friend, rather than a dependent.

As the day was showery, Scott was attended by one of his retainers, named Tommie Purdie, who carried his plaid, and who deserves especial mention. Sophia Scott used to call him her father's grand vizier, and she gave a playful account one evening, as she was hanging on her father's arm, of the consultations which he and Tommie used to have about matters relative to farming. Purdie was tenacious of his opinions, and he and Scott would have long disputes in front of the house, as to something that was to be done on the estate, until the latter, fairly tired out, would abandon the ground and the argument, exclaiming, "Well, well, Tom, have it your own way."

After a time, however, Purdie would present himself at the door of the parlor, and observe, "I ha' been thinking over the matter, and upon the whole, I think I'll take your honor's advice."

Scott laughed heartily when this anecdote was told of him. "It was with him and Tom," he said, "as it was with an old laird and a pet servant, whom he had indulged until he was positive beyond all endurance." "This won't do!" cried the old laird, in a passion, "we can't live together any longer--we must part." "An' where the deil does your honor mean to go?" replied the other.

I would, moreover, observe of Tom Purdie, that he was a firm believer in ghosts, and warlocks, and all kinds of old wives' fable. He was a religious man, too, mingling a little degree of Scottish pride in his devotion; for though his salary was but twenty pounds a year, he had managed to afford seven pounds for a family Bible. It is true, he had one hundred pounds clear of the world, and was looked up to by his comrades as a man of property.

In the course of our morning's walk, we stopped at a small house belonging to one of the laborers on the estate. The object of Scott's visit was to inspect a relic which had been digged up in a Roman camp, and which, if I recollect right, he pronounced to have been a tongs. It was produced by the cottager's wife, a ruddy, healthy-looking dame, whom Scott addressed by the name of Ailie. As he stood regarding the relic, turning it round and round, and making comments upon it, half grave, half comic, with the cottage group around him, all joining occasionally in the colloquy, the inimitable character of Monkbarns was again brought to mind, and I seemed to see before me that prince of antiquarians and humorists holding forth to his unlearned and unbelieving neighbors.

Whenever Scott touched, in this way, upon local antiquities, and in all his familiar conversations about local traditions and superstitions, there was always a sly and quiet humor running at the bottom of his discourse, and playing about his countenance, as if he sported with the subject. It seemed to me as if he distrusted his own enthusiasm, and was disposed to droll upon his own humors and peculiarities, yet, at the same time, a poetic gleam in his eye would show that he really took a strong relish and interest in them. "It was a pity," he said, "that antiquarians were generally so dry, for the subjects they handled were rich in historical and poetical recollections, in picturesque details, in quaint and heroic characteristics, and in all kinds of curious and obsolete ceremonials. They are always groping among the rarest materials for poetry, but they have no idea of turning them to poetic use. Now every fragment from old times has, in some degree, its story with it, or gives an inkling of something characteristic of the circumstances and manners of its day, and so sets the imagination at work."

For my own part I never met with antiquarian so delightful, either in his writings or his conversation; and the quiet sub-acid humor that was prone to mingle in his disquisitions, gave them, to me, a peculiar and an exquisite flavor. But he seemed, in fact, to undervalue everything that concerned himself. The play of his genius was so easy that he was unconscious of its mighty power, and made light of those sports of intellect that shamed the efforts and labors of other minds.

Our ramble this morning took us again up the Rhymer's Glen, and by

Huntley Bank, and Huntley Wood, and the silver waterfall overhung with weeping birches and mountain ashes, those delicate and beautiful trees which grace the green shaws and burnsides of Scotland. The heather, too, that closely woven robe of Scottish landscape which covers the nakedness of its hills and mountains, tinted the neighborhood with soft and rich colors. As we ascended the glen, the prospects opened upon us; Melrose, with its towers and pinnacles, lay below; beyond were the Eildon hills, the Cowden Knowes, the Tweed, the Galla Water, and all the storied vicinity; the whole landscape varied by gleams of sunshine and driving showers.

Scott, as usual, took the lead, limping along with great activity, and in joyous mood, giving scraps of border rhymes and border stories; two or three times in the course of our walk there were drizzling showers, which I supposed would put an end to our ramble, but my companions trudged on as unconcernedly as if it had been fine weather.

At length, I asked whether we had not better seek some shelter. "True," said Scott, "I did not recollect that you were not accustomed to our Scottish mists. This is a lachrymose climate, evermore showering. We, however, are children of the mist, and must not mind a little whimpering of the clouds any more than a man must mind the weeping of an hysterical wife. As you are not accustomed to be wet through, as a matter of course, in a morning's walk, we will bide a bit under the lee of this bank until the shower is over." Taking his seat under shelter of a thicket, he called to his man George for his tartan, then turning to me, "Come," said he, "come under my plaidy, as the old song goes;" so, making me nestle down beside him, he wrapped a part of the plaid round me, and took me, as he said, under his wing. While we were thus nestled together, he pointed to a hole in the opposite bank of the glen. That, he said, was the hole of an old gray badger, who was doubtless snugly housed in this bad weather. Sometimes he saw him at the entrance of his hole, like a hermit at the door of his cell, telling his beads, or reading a homily. He had a great respect for the venerable anchorite, and would not suffer him to be disturbed. He was a kind of successor to Thomas the Rhymer, and perhaps might be Thomas himself returned from fairy land, but still under fairy spell.

Some accident turned the conversation upon Hogg, the poet, in which Laidlaw, who was seated beside us, took a part. Hogg had once been a shepherd in the service of his father, and Laidlaw gave many interesting anecdotes of him, of which I now retain no recollection. They used to tend the sheep together when Laidlaw was a boy, and Hogg would recite the first struggling conceptions of his muse. At night when Laidlaw was quartered comfortably in bed, in the farmhouse, poor Hogg would take to the shepherd's hut in the field on the hillside, and there lie awake for hours together, and look at the stars and make poetry, which he would repeat the next day to his companion.

Scott spoke in warm terms of Hogg, and repeated passages from his beautiful poem of "Kelmeny," to which he gave great and well-merited praise. He gave, also, some amusing anecdotes of Hogg and his publisher, Blackwood, who was at that time just rising into the bibliographical importance which he has since enjoyed.

Hogg, in one of his poems, I believe the "Pilgrims of the Sun," had dabbled a little in metaphysics, and like his heroes, had got into the clouds. Blackwood, who began to affect criticism, argued stoutly with him as to the necessity of omitting or elucidating some obscure passage. Hogg was immovable.

"But, man," said Blackwood, "I dinna ken what ye mean in this passage." "Hout tout, man," replied Hogg, impatiently, "I dinna ken always what I mean mysel." There is many a metaphysical poet in the same predicament with honest Hogg.

Scott promised to invite the Shepherd to Abbotsford during my visit, and I anticipated much gratification in meeting with him, from the account I had received of his character and manners, and the great pleasure I had derived from his works. Circumstances, however, prevented Scott from performing his promise; and to my great regret I left Scotland without seeing one of its most original and national characters.

When the weather held up, we continued our walk until we came to a beautiful sheet of water, in the bosom of the mountain, called, if I recollect right, the lake of Cauldshiel. Scott prided himself much upon this little Mediterranean sea in his dominions, and hoped I was not too much spoiled by our great lakes in America to relish it. He proposed to take me out to the centre of it, to a fine point of view, for which purpose we embarked in a small boat, which had been put on the lake by his neighbor, Lord Somerville. As I was about to step on board, I observed in large letters on one of the benches, "Search No. 2." I paused for a moment and repeated the inscription aloud, trying to recollect something I had heard or read to which it alluded. "Pshaw," cried Scott, "it is only some of Lord Somerville's nonsense--get in!" In an instant scenes in the Antiquary connected with "Search No. 1," flashed upon my mind. "Ah! I remember now," said I, and with a laugh took my seat, but adverted no more to the circumstance.

We had a pleasant row about the lake, which commanded some pretty scenery. The most interesting circumstance connected with it, however, according to Scott, was, that it was haunted by a bogle in the shape of a water bull, which lived in the deep parts, and now and then came forth upon dry land and made a tremendous roaring, that shook the very hills. This story had been current in the vicinity from time immemorial;--there was a man living who declared he had seen the bull, --and he was believed by many of his simple neighbors. "I don't choose to contradict the tale," said Scott, "for I am willing to have my lake stocked with any fish, flesh, or fowl that my neighbors think proper to put into it; and these old wives' fables are a kind of property in Scotland that belongs to the estates and goes with the soil. Our streams and lochs are like the rivers and pools in Germany, that have all their Wasser Nixe, or water witches, and I have a fancy for these kind of amphibious bogles and hobgoblins."

*   *   *   *   *

Scott went on after we had landed to make many remarks, mingled with picturesque anecdotes, concerning the fabulous beings with which the Scotch were apt to people the wild streams and lochs that occur in the solemn and lonely scenes of their mountains; and to compare them with similar superstitions among the northern nations of Europe; but Scotland, he said, was above all other countries for this wild and vivid progeny of the fancy, from the nature of the scenery, the misty magnificence and vagueness of the climate, the wild and gloomy events of its history; the clannish divisions of its people; their local feelings, notions, and prejudices; the individuality of their dialect, in which all kinds of odd and peculiar notions were incorporated; by the secluded life of their mountaineers; the lonely habits of their pastoral people, much of whose time was passed on the solitary hillsides; their traditional songs, which clothed every rock and stream with old world stories, handed down from age to age, and generation to generation. The Scottish mind, he said, was made up of poetry and strong common sense; and the very strength of the latter gave perpetuity and luxuriance to the former. It was a strong tenacious soil, into which, when once a seed of poetry fell, it struck deep root and brought forth abundantly. "You will never weed these popular stories and songs and superstitions out of Scotland," said he. "It is not so much that the people believe in them, as that they delight in them. They belong to the native hills and streams of which they are fond, and to the history of their forefathers, of which they are proud."

"It would do your heart good," continued he, "to see a number of our poor country people seated round the ingle nook, which is generally capacious enough, and passing the long dark dreary winter nights listening to some old wife, or strolling gaberlunzie, dealing out auld world stories about bogles and warlocks, or about raids and forays, and border skirmishes; or reciting some ballad stuck full of those fighting names that stir up a true Scotchman's blood like the sound of a trumpet. These traditional tales and ballads have lived for ages in mere oral circulation, being passed from father to son, or rather from grandam to grandchild, and are a kind of hereditary property of the poor peasantry, of which it would be hard to deprive them, as they have not circulating libraries to supply them with works of fiction in their place."

I do not pretend to give the precise words, but, as nearly as I can from scanty memorandums and vague recollections, the leading ideas of Scott. I am constantly sensible, however, how far I fall short of his copiousness and richness.

He went on to speak of the elves and sprites, so frequent in Scottish legend. "Our fairies, however," said he, "though they dress in green, and gambol by moonlight about the banks, and shaws, and burnsides, are not such pleasant little folks as the English fairies, but are apt to bear more of the warlock in their natures, and to play spiteful tricks. When I was a boy, I used to look wistfully at the green hillocks that were said to be haunted by fairies, and felt sometimes as if I should like to lie down by them and sleep, and be carried off to Fairy Land, only that I did not like some of the cantrips which used now and then to be played off upon visitors."

Here Scott recounted, in graphic style, and with much humor, a little

story which used to be current in the neighborhood, of an honest
burgess of Selkirk, who, being at work upon the hill of Peatlaw, fell
asleep upon one of these "fairy knowes," or hillocks. When he awoke, he
rubbed his eyes and gazed about him with astonishment, for he was in
the market-place of a great city, with a crowd of people bustling about
him, not one of whom he knew. At length he accosted a bystander, and
asked him the name of the place. "Hout man," replied the other, "are ye
in the heart o' Glasgow, and speer the name of it?" The poor man was
astonished, and would not believe either ears or eyes; he insisted that
he had lain down to sleep but half an hour before on the Peatlaw, near
Selkirk. He came well-nigh being taken up for a madman, when,
fortunately, a Selkirk man came by, who knew him, and took charge of
him, and conducted him back to his native place. Here, however, he was
likely to fare no better, when he spoke of having been whisked in his
sleep from the Peatlaw to Glasgow. The truth of the matter at length
came out; his coat, which he had taken off when at work on the Peatlaw,
was found lying near a "fairy knowe," and his bonnet, which was
missing, was discovered on the weathercock of Lanark steeple. So it was
as clear as day that he had been carried through the air by the fairies
while he was sleeping, and his bonnet had been blown off by the way.

I give this little story but meagrely from a scanty memorandum; Scott
has related it in somewhat different style in a note to one of his
poems; but in narration these anecdotes derived their chief zest, from
the quiet but delightful humor, the bonhomie with which he seasoned
them, and the sly glance of the eye from under his bushy eyebrows, with
which they were accompanied. That day at dinner, we had Mr. Laidlaw and
his wife, and a female friend who accompanied them. The latter was a
very intelligent, respectable person, about the middle age, and was
treated with particular attention and courtesy by Scott. Our dinner was
a most agreeable one; for the guests were evidently cherished visitors
to the house, and felt that they were appreciated.

When they were gone, Scott spoke of them in the most cordial manner. "I wished to show you," said he, "some of our really excellent, plain Scotch people; not fine gentlemen and ladies, for such you can meet everywhere, and they are everywhere the same. The character of a nation is not to be learnt from its fine folks."

He then went on with a particular eulogium on the lady who had accompanied the Laidlaws. She was the daughter, he said, of a poor country clergyman, who had died in debt, and left her an orphan and destitute. Having had a good plain education, she immediately set up a child's school, and had soon a numerous flock under her care, by which she earned a decent maintenance. That, however, was not her main object. Her first care was to pay off her father's debts, that no ill word or ill will might rest upon his memory.

This, by dint of Scottish economy, backed by filial reverence and pride, she accomplished, though in the effort, she subjected herself to every privation. Not content with this, she in certain instances refused to take pay for the tuition of the children of some of her neighbors, who had befriended her father in his need, and had since fallen into poverty. "In a word," added Scott, "she is a fine old Scotch girl; and I delight in her, more than in many a fine lady I have known, and I have known many of the finest."

＊　　＊　　＊　　＊　　＊

It is time, however, to draw this rambling narrative to a close. Several days were passed by me, in the way I have attempted to describe, in almost constant, familiar, and joyous conversation with Scott; it was as if I were admitted to a social communion with Shakespeare, for it was with one of a kindred, if not equal genius. Every night I retired with my mind filled with delightful recollections of the day, and every morning I rose with the certainty of new enjoyment. The days thus spent, I shall ever look back to, as among the very happiest of my life; for I was conscious at the time of being happy. The only sad moment that I experienced at Abbotsford was that of my departure; but it was cheered with the prospect of soon returning; for I had promised, after making a tour in the Highlands, to come and pass a few more days on the banks of the Tweed, when Scott intended to invite Hogg the poet to meet me. I took a kind farewell of the family, with each of whom I had been highly pleased. If I have refrained from dwelling particularly on their several characters, and giving anecdotes of them individually, it is because I consider them shielded by the sanctity of domestic life; Scott, on the contrary, belongs to history. As he accompanied me on foot, however, to a small gate on the confines of his premises, I could not refrain from expressing the enjoyment I had experienced in his domestic circle, and passing some warm eulogiums on the young folks from whom I had just parted. I shall never forget his reply. "They have kind hearts," said he, "and that is the main point as to human happiness. They love one another, poor things, which is every thing in domestic life. The best wish I can make you, my friend," added he, laying his hand upon my shoulder, "is, that when you return to your own country, you may get married, and have a family of young bairns about you. If you are happy, there they are to share your happiness--and if you are otherwise--there they are to comfort you."

By this time we had reached the gate, when he halted, and took my hand. "I will not say farewell," said he, "for it is always a painful word, but I will say, come again. When you have made your tour to the Highlands, come here and give me a few more days--but come when you please, you will always find Abbotsford open to you, and a hearty welcome."

*   *   *   *   *

I have thus given, in a rude style, my main recollections of what occurred during my sojourn at Abbotsford, and I feel mortified that I can give but such meagre, scattered, and colorless details of what was so copious, rich, and varied. During several days that I passed there Scott was in admirable vein. From early morn until dinner time he was rambling about, showing me the neighborhood, and during dinner and until late at night, engaged in social conversation. No time was reserved for himself; he seemed as if his only occupation was to entertain me; and yet I was almost an entire stranger to him, one of whom he knew nothing, but an idle book I had written, and which, some years before, had amused him. But such was Scott--he appeared to have nothing to do but lavish his time, attention, and conversation on those around. It was difficult to imagine what time he found to write those volumes that were incessantly issuing from the press; all of which, too, were of a nature to require reading and research. I could not find that his life was ever otherwise than a life of leisure and haphazard recreation, such as it was during my visit. He scarce ever balked a party of pleasure, or a sporting excursion, and rarely pleaded his own concerns as an excuse for rejecting those of others. During my visit I heard of other visitors who had preceded me, and who must have kept him occupied for many days, and I have had an opportunity of knowing the course of his daily life for some time subsequently. Not long after my departure from Abbotsford, my friend Wilkie arrived there, to paint a picture of the Scott family. He found the house full of guests. Scott's whole time was taken up in riding and driving about the country, or in social conversation at home. "All this time," said Wilkie to me, "I did not presume to ask Mr. Scott to sit for his portrait, for I saw he had not a moment to spare; I waited for the guests to go away, but as fast as one went another arrived, and so it continued for several days, and with each set he was completely occupied. At length all went off, and we were quiet. I thought, however, Mr. Scott will now shut himself up among his books and papers, for he has to make up for lost time; it won't do for me to ask him now to sit for his picture. Laidlaw, who managed his estate, came in, and Scott turned to him, as I supposed, to consult about business. 'Laidlaw,' said he, 'to-morrow morning we'll go across the water and take the dogs with us--there's a place where I think we shall be able to find a hare.'

"In short," added Wilkie, "I found that instead of business, he was thinking only of amusement, as if he had nothing in the world to occupy him; so I no longer feared to intrude upon him."

The conversation of Scott was frank, hearty, picturesque, and dramatic. During the time of my visit he inclined to the comic rather than the grave, in his anecdotes and stories, and such, I was told, was his general inclination. He relished a joke, or a trait of humor in social intercourse, and laughed with right good will. He talked not for effect nor display, but from the flow of his spirits, the stores of his memory, and the vigor of his imagination. He had a natural turn for narration, and his narratives and descriptions were without effort, yet wonderfully graphic. He placed the scene before you like a picture; he gave the dialogue with the appropriate dialect or peculiarities, and described the appearance and characters of his personages with that spirit and felicity evinced in his writings. Indeed, his conversation reminded me continually of his novels; and it seemed to me, that during the whole time I was with him., he talked enough to fill volumes, and that they could not have been filled more delightfully.

He was as good a listener as talker, appreciating everything that others said, however humble might be their rank or pretensions, and was quick to testify his perception of any point in their discourse. He arrogated nothing to himself, but was perfectly unassuming and unpretending, entering with heart and soul into the business, or pleasure, or, I had almost said, folly, of the hour and the company. No one's concerns, no one's thoughts, no one's opinions, no one's tastes and pleasures seemed beneath him. He made himself so thoroughly the companion of those with whom he happened to be, that they forgot for a time his vast superiority, and only recollected and wondered, when all was over, that it was Scott with whom they had been on such familiar terms, and in whose society they had felt so perfectly at their ease.

It was delightful to observe the generous spirit in which he spoke of all his literary contemporaries, quoting the beauties of their works, and this, too, with respect to persons with whom he might have been supposed to be at variance in literature or politics. Jeffrey, it was thought, had ruffled his plumes in one of his reviews, yet Scott spoke of him in terms of high and warm eulogy, both as an author and as a man.

His humor in conversation, as in his works, was genial and free from all causticity. He had a quick perception of faults and foibles, but he looked upon poor human nature with an indulgent eye, relishing what was good and pleasant, tolerating what was frail, and pitying what was evil. It is this beneficent spirit which gives such an air of bonhomie to Scott's humor throughout all his works. He played with the foibles and errors of his fellow beings, and presented them in a thousand whimsical and characteristic lights, but the kindness and generosity of his nature would not allow him to be a satirist. I do not recollect a sneer throughout his conversation any more than there is throughout his works.

Such is a rough sketch of Scott, as I saw him in private life, not merely at the time of the visit here narrated, but in the casual intercourse of subsequent years. Of his public character and merits, all the world can judge. His works have incorporated themselves with the thoughts and concerns of the whole civilized world, for a quarter of a century, and have had a controlling influence over the age in which he lived. But when did a human being ever exercise an influence more salutary and benignant? Who is there that, on looking back over a great portion of his life, does not find the genius of Scott administering to his pleasures, beguiling his cares, and soothing his lonely sorrows? Who does not still regard his works as a treasury of pure enjoyment, an armory to which to resort in time of need, to find weapons with which to fight off the evils and the griefs of life? For my own part, in periods of dejection, I have hailed the announcement of a new work from his pen as an earnest of certain pleasure in store for me, and have looked forward to it as a traveller in a waste looks to a green spot at a distance, where he feels assured of solace and refreshment. When I consider how much he has thus contributed to the better hours of my past existence, and how independent his works still make me, at times, of all the world for my enjoyment, I bless my stars that cast my lot in his days, to be thus cheered and gladdened by the outpourings of his genius. I consider it one of the greatest advantages that I have derived from my literary career, that it has elevated me into genial communion with such a spirit; and as a tribute of gratitude for his friendship, and veneration for his memory, I cast this humble stone upon his cairn, which will soon, I trust, be piled aloft with the contributions of abler hands.

NEWSTEAD ABBEY

HISTORICAL NOTICE.

Being about to give a few sketches taken during a three weeks' sojourn in the ancestral mansion of the late Lord Byron, I think it proper to premise some brief particulars concerning its history.

Newstead Abbey is one of the finest specimens in existence of those quaint and romantic piles, half castle, half convent, which remain as monuments of the olden times of England. It stands, too, in the midst of a legendary neighborhood; being in the heart of Sherwood Forest, and surrounded by the haunts of Robin Hood and his band of outlaws, so famous in ancient ballad and nursery tale. It is true, the forest scarcely exists but in name, and the tract of country over which it once extended its broad solitudes and shades, is now an open and smiling region, cultivated with parks and farms, and enlivened with villages.

Newstead, which probably once exerted a monastic sway over this region, and controlled the consciences of the rude foresters, was originally a priory, founded in the latter part of the twelfth century, by Henry II., at the time when he sought, by building of shrines and convents, and by other acts of external piety, to expiate the murder of Thomas a Becket. The priory was dedicated to God and the Virgin, and was inhabited by a fraternity of canons regular of St. Augustine. This order was originally simple and abstemious in its mode of living, and exemplary in its conduct; but it would seem that it gradually lapsed into those abuses which disgraced too many of the wealthy monastic establishments; for there are documents among its archives which intimate the prevalence of gross misrule and dissolute sensuality among its members. At the time of the dissolution of the convents during the reign of Henry VIII., Newstead underwent a sudden reverse, being given, with the neighboring manor and rectory of Papelwick, to Sir John Byron, Steward of Manchester and Rochdale, and Lieutenant of Sherwood Forest. This ancient family worthy figures in the traditions of the Abbey, and in the ghost stories with which it abounds, under the quaint and graphic appellation of "Sir John Byron the Little, with the great Beard." He converted the saintly edifice into a castellated dwelling, making it his favorite residence and the seat of his forest jurisdiction.

The Byron family being subsequently ennobled by a baronial title, and enriched by various possessions, maintained great style and retinue at Newstead. The proud edifice partook, however, of the vicissitudes of the times, and Lord Byron, in one of his poems, represents it as alternately the scene of lordly wassailing and of civil war:

"Hark, how the hall resounding to the strain,
  Shakes with the martial music's novel din!
The heralds of a warrior's haughty reign,
  High crested banners wave thy walls within.

"Of changing sentinels the distant hum,
  The mirth of feasts, the clang of burnish'd arms,
The braying trumpet, and the hoarser drum,
  Unite in concert with increased alarms."

About the middle of the last century, the Abbey came into the possession of another noted character, who makes no less figure in its shadowy traditions than Sir John the Little with the great Beard. This was the grand-uncle of the poet, familiarly known among the gossiping chroniclers of the Abbey as "the Wicked Lord Byron." He is represented as a man of irritable passions and vindictive temper, in the indulgence of which an incident occurred which gave a turn to his whole character and life, and in some measure affected the fortunes of the Abbey. In his neighborhood lived his kinsman and friend, Mr. Chaworth, proprietor of Annesley Hall. Being together in London in 1765, in a chamber of the Star and Garter tavern in Pall Mall, a quarrel rose between them. Byron insisted upon settling it upon the spot by single combat. They fought without seconds, by the dim light of a candle, and Mr. Chaworth, although the most expert swordsman, received a mortal wound. With his dying breath he related such particulars the contest as induced the coroner's jury to return a verdict of wilful murder. Lord Byron was sent to the Tower, and subsequently tried before the House of Peers, where an ultimate verdict was given of manslaughter.

He retired after this to the Abbey, where he shut himself up to brood over his disgraces; grew gloomy, morose, and fantastical, and indulged in fits of passion and caprice, that made him the theme of rural wonder and scandal. No tale was too wild or too monstrous for vulgar belief. Like his successor the poet, he was accused of all kinds of vagaries and wickedness. It was said that he always went armed, as if prepared to commit murder on the least provocation. At one time, when a gentleman of his neighborhood was to dine *tete a tete* with him, it is said a brace of pistols were gravely laid with the knives and forks upon the table, as part of the regular table furniture, and implements that might be needed in the course of the repast. Another rumor states that being exasperated at his coachman for disobedience to orders, he shot him on the spot, threw his body into the coach where Lady Byron was seated, and, mounting the box, officiated in his stead. At another time, according to the same vulgar rumors, he threw her ladyship into the lake in front of the Abbey, where she would have been drowned, but for the timely aid of the gardener. These stories are doubtless exaggerations of trivial incidents which may have occurred; but it is certain that the wayward passions of this unhappy man caused a separation from his wife, and finally spread a solitude around him. Being displeased at the marriage of his son and heir, he displayed an inveterate malignity toward him. Not being able to cut off his succession to the Abbey estate, which descended to him by entail, he endeavored to injure it as much as possible, so that it might come a mere wreck into his hands. For this purpose he suffered the Abbey to fall out of repair, and everything to go to waste about it, and cut down all the timber on the estate, laying low many a tract of old Sherwood Forest, so that the Abbey lands lay stripped and bare of all their ancient honors. He was baffled in his unnatural revenge by the premature death of his son, and passed the remainder of his days in his deserted and dilapidated halls, a gloomy misanthrope, brooding amidst the scenes he had laid desolate.

His wayward humors drove from him all neighborly society, and for a part of the time he was almost without domestics. In his misanthropic mood, when at variance with all human kind, he took to feeding crickets, so that in process of time the Abbey was overrun with them, and its lonely halls made more lonely at night by their monotonous music. Tradition adds that, at his death, the crickets seemed aware that they had lost their patron and protector, for they one and all packed up bag and baggage, and left the Abbey, trooping across its courts and corridors in all directions.

The death of the "Old Lord," or "The Wicked Lord Byron," for he is known by both appellations, occurred in 1798; and the Abbey then passed into the possession of the poet. The latter was but eleven years of age, and living in humble style with his mother in Scotland. They came soon after to England, to take possession. Moore gives a simple but striking anecdote of the first arrival of the poet at the domains of his ancestors.

They had arrived at the Newstead toll-bar, and saw the woods of the Abbey stretching out to receive them, when Mrs. Byron, affecting to be ignorant of the place, asked the woman of the toll-house to whom that seat belonged? She was told that the owner of it, Lord Byron, had been some months dead. "And who is the next heir?" asked the proud and happy mother. "They say," answered the old woman, "it is a little boy who lives at Aberdeen." "And this is he, bless him!" exclaimed the nurse, no longer able to contain herself, and turning to kiss with delight the young lord who was seated on her lap. [Note: Moore's Life of Lord Byron.]

During Lord Byron's minority, the Abbey was let to Lord Grey de Ruthen, but the poet visited it occasionally during the Harrow vacations, when he resided with his mother at lodgings in Nottingham. It was treated

little better by its present tenant, than by the old lord who preceded
him; so that when, in the autumn of 1808, Lord Byron took up his abode
there, it was in a ruinous condition. The following lines from his own
pen may give some idea of its condition:

"Through thy battlements, Newstead. the hollow winds whistle,
  Thou, the hall of my fathers, art gone to decay;
 In thy once smiling garden, the hemlock and thistle
  Have choked up the rose which once bloomed in the way.

"Of the mail-covered barons who, proudly, to battle
  Led thy vassals from Europe to Palestine's plain,
 The escutcheon and shield, which with every wind rattle,
  Are the only sad vestiges now that remain."

[Note: Lines on leaving Newstead Abbey.]

In another poem he expresses the melancholy feeling with which he took
possession of his ancestral mansion:

"Newstead! what saddening scene of change is thine,
  Thy yawning arch betokens sure decay:
 The last and youngest of a noble line,
  Now holds thy mouldering turrets in his sway.

"Deserted now, he scans thy gray-worn towers,
  Thy vaults, where dead of feudal ages sleep,
 Thy cloisters, pervious to the wintry showers,
  These--these he views, and views them but to weep.

"Yet he prefers thee to the gilded domes,
  Or gewgaw grottoes of the vainly great;
 Yet lingers mid thy damp and mossy tombs,

Nor breathes a murmur 'gainst the will of fate."

[Note: Elegy on Newstead Abbey.]

Lord Byron had not fortune sufficient to put the pile in extensive repair, nor to maintain anything like the state of his ancestors. He restored some of the apartments, so as to furnish his mother with a comfortable habitation, and fitted up a quaint study for himself, in which, among books and busts, and other library furniture, were two skulls of the ancient friars, grinning on each side of an antique cross. One of his gay companions gives a picture of Newstead when thus repaired, and the picture is sufficiently desolate.

"There are two tiers of cloisters, with a variety of cells and rooms about them, which, though not inhabited, nor in an inhabitable state, might easily be made so; and many of the original rooms, among which is a fine stone hall, are still in use. Of the Abbey church, one end only remains; and the old kitchen, with a long range of apartments, is reduced to a heap of rubbish. Leading from the Abbey to the modern part of the habitation is a noble room, seventy feet in length, and twenty-three in breadth; but every part of the house displays neglect and decay, save those which the present lord has lately fitted up." [Note: Letter of the late Charles Skinner Mathews, Esq.]

Even the repairs thus made were but of transient benefit, for the roof being left in its dilapidated state, the rain soon penetrated into the apartments which Lord Byron had restored and decorated, and in a few years rendered them almost as desolate as the rest of the Abbey.

Still he felt a pride in the ruinous old edifice; its very dreary and dismantled state, addressed itself to his poetical imagination, and to that love of the melancholy and the grand which is evinced in all his writings. "Come what may," said he in one of his letters, "Newstead and

I stand or fall together. I have now lived on the spot. I have fixed my heart upon it, and no pressure, present or future, shall induce me to barter the last vestige of our inheritance. I have that pride within me which will enable me to support difficulties: could I obtain in exchange for Newstead Abbey, the first fortune in the country, I would reject the proposition."

His residence at the Abbey, however, was fitful and uncertain. He passed occasional portions of time there, sometimes studiously and alone, oftener idly and recklessly, and occasionally with young and gay companions, in riot and revelry, and the indulgence of all kinds of mad caprice. The Abbey was by no means benefited by these roystering inmates, who sometimes played off monkish mummeries about the cloisters, at other times turned the state chambers into schools for boxing and single-stick, and shot pistols in the great hall. The country people of the neighborhood were as much puzzled by these madcap vagaries of the new incumbent, as by the gloomier habits of the "old lord," and began to think that madness was inherent in the Byron race, or that some wayward star ruled over the Abbey.

It is needless to enter into a detail of the circumstances which led his Lordship to sell his ancestral estate, notwithstanding the partial predilections and hereditary feeling which he had so eloquently expressed. Fortunately, it fell into the hands of a man who possessed something of a poetical temperament, and who cherished an enthusiastic admiration for Lord Byron. Colonel (at that time Major) Wildman had been a schoolmate of the poet, and sat with him on the same form at Harrow. He had subsequently distinguished himself in the war of the Peninsula, and at the battle of Waterloo, and it was a great consolation to Lord Byron, in parting with his family estate, to know that it would be held by one capable of restoring its faded glories, and who would respect and preserve all the monuments and memorials of his line. [Note: The following letter, written in the course of the transfer of the estate, has never been published:--

Venice, November 18, 1818.

My Dear Wildman,

Mr. Hanson is on the eve of his return, so that I have only time to return a few inadequate thanks for your very kind letter. I should regret to trouble you with any requests of mine, in regard to the preservation of any signs of my family, which may still exist at Newstead, and leave everything of that kind to your own feelings, present or future, upon the subject. The portrait which you flatter me by desiring, would not be worth to you your trouble and expense of such an expedition, but you may rely upon having the very first that may be painted, and which may seem worth your acceptance.

I trust that Newstead will, being yours, remain so, and that it may see you as happy, as I am very sure that you will make your dependents. With regard to myself, you may be sure that whether in the fourth, or fifth, or sixth form at Harrow, or in the fluctuations of after life, I shall always remember with regard my old schoolfellow--fellow monitor, and friend, and recognize with respect the gallant soldier, who, with all the advantages of fortune and allurements of youth to a life of pleasure, devoted himself to duties of a nobler order, and will receive his reward in the esteem and admiration of his country.

Ever yours most truly and affectionately,
  BYRON.]

The confidence of Lord Byron in the good feeling and good taste of Colonel Wildman has been justified by the event. Under his judicious eye and munificent hand the venerable and romantic pile has risen from its ruins in all its old monastic and baronial splendor, and additions have been made to it in perfect conformity of style. The groves and forests have been replanted; the lakes and fish-ponds cleaned out, and the gardens rescued from the "hemlock and thistle," and restored to their pristine and dignified formality.

The farms on the estate have been put in complete order, new farm-houses built of stone, in the picturesque and comfortable style of the old English granges; the hereditary tenants secured in their paternal homes, and treated with the most considerate indulgence; everything, in a word, gives happy indications of a liberal and beneficent landlord.

What most, however, will interest the visitors to the Abbey in favor of its present occupant, is the reverential care with which he has preserved and renovated every monument and relic of the Byron family, and every object in anywise connected with the memory of the poet. Eighty thousand pounds have already been expended upon the venerable pile, yet the work is still going on, and Newstead promises to realize the hope faintly breathed by the poet when bidding it a melancholy farewell--

"Haply thy sun emerging, yet may shine,
  Thee to irradiate with meridian ray;
Hours splendid as the past may still be thine,
  And bless thy future, as thy former day."

ARRIVAL AT THE ABBEY.

I had been passing a merry Christmas in the good old style at Barlhoro' Hall, a venerable family mansion in Derbyshire, and set off to finish the holidays with the hospitable proprietor of Newstead Abbey. A drive of seventeen miles through a pleasant country, part of it the storied region of Sherwood Forest, brought me to the gate of Newstead Park. The aspect of the park was by no means imposing, the fine old trees that once adorned it having been laid low by Lord Byron's wayward predecessor.

Entering the gate, the postchaise rolled heavily along a sandy road, between naked declivities, gradually descending into one of those gentle and sheltered valleys, in which the sleek monks of old loved to nestle themselves. Here a sweep of the road round an angle of a garden wall brought us full in front of the venerable edifice, embosomed in the valley, with a beautiful sheet of water spreading out before it.

The irregular gray pile, of motley architecture, answered to the description given by Lord Byron:

> "An old, old monastery once, and now
> Still older mansion, of a rich and rare
> Mixed Gothic"----

One end was fortified by a castellated tower, bespeaking the baronial and warlike days of the edifice; the other end maintained its primitive monastic character. A ruined chapel, flanked by a solemn grove, still reared its front entire. It is true, the threshold of the once frequented portal was grass-grown, and the great lancet window, once glorious with painted glass, was now entwined and overhung with ivy; but the old convent cross still braved both time and tempest on the pinnacle of the chapel, and below, the blessed effigies of the Virgin and child, sculptured in gray stone, remained uninjured in their niche, giving a sanctified aspect to the pile. [Note:

> "--in a higher niche, alone, but crown'd,

The Virgin Mother of the God-born child
With her son in her blessed arms, looked round,
  Spared by some chance, when all beside was spoil'd:
She made the earth below seem holy ground."--DON JUAN, Canto III.]

A flight of rooks, tenants of the adjacent grove, were hovering about the ruin, and balancing themselves upon ever airy projection, and looked down with curious eye and cawed as the postchaise rattled along below.

The chamberlain of the Abbey, a most decorous personage, dressed in black, received us at the portal. Here, too, we encountered a memento of Lord Byron, a great black and white Newfoundland dog, that had accompanied his remains from Greece. He was descended from the famous Boatswain, and inherited his generous qualities. He was a cherished inmate of the Abbey, and honored and caressed by every visitor. Conducted by the chamberlain, and followed by the dog, who assisted in doing the honors of the house, we passed through a long low vaulted hall, supported by massive Gothic arches, and not a little resembling the crypt of a cathedral, being the basement story of the Abbey.

From this we ascended a stone staircase, at the head of which a pair of folding doors admitted us into a broad corridor that ran round the interior of the Abbey. The windows of the corridor looked into a quadrangular grass-grown court, forming the hollow centre of the pile. In the midst of it rose a lofty and fantastic fountain, wrought of the same gray stone as the main edifice, and which has been well described by Lord Byron.

"Amidst the court a Gothic fountain play'd,
  Symmetrical, but deck'd with carvings quaint,
Strange faces, like to men in masquerade,
  And here perhaps a monster, there a saint:

The spring rush'd through grim mouths of granite made,
　And sparkled into basins, where it spent
Its little torrent in a thousand bubbles,
Like man's vain glory, and his vainer troubles."

[Note: DON JUAN, Canto III]

Around this quadrangle were low vaulted cloisters, with Gothic arches, once the secluded walks of the monks: the corridor along which we were passing was built above these cloisters, and their hollow arches seemed to reverberate every footfall. Everything thus far had a solemn monastic air; but, on arriving at an angle of the corridor, the eye, glancing along a shadowy gallery, caught a sight of two dark figures in plate armor, with closed visors, bucklers braced, and swords drawn, standing motionless against the wall. They seemed two phantoms of the chivalrous era of the Abbey.

Here the chamberlain, throwing open a folding door, ushered us at once into a spacious and lofty saloon, which offered a brilliant contrast to the quaint and sombre apartments we had traversed. It was elegantly furnished, and the walls hung with paintings, yet something of its original architecture had been preserved and blended with modern embellishments. There were the stone-shafted casements and the deep bow-window of former times. The carved and panelled wood-work of the lofty ceiling had likewise been carefully restored, and its Gothic and grotesque devices painted and gilded in their ancient style.

Here, too, were emblems of the former and latter days of the Abbey, in the effigies of the first and last of the Byron line that held sway over its destinies. At the upper end of the saloon, above the door, the dark Gothic portrait of "Sir John Byron the Little with the great Beard," looked grimly down from his canvas, while, at the opposite end, a white marble bust of the ***genius loci***, the noble poet, shone conspicuously from its pedestal.

The whole air and style of the apartment partook more of the palace than the monastery, and its windows looked forth on a suitable prospect, composed of beautiful groves, smooth verdant lawns, and silver sheets of water. Below the windows was a small flower-garden, inclosed by stone balustrades, on which were stately peacocks, sunning themselves and displaying their plumage. About the grass-plots in front, were gay cock pheasants, and plump partridges, and nimble-footed water hens, feeding almost in perfect security.

Such was the medley of objects presented to the eye on first visiting the Abbey, and I found the interior fully to answer the description of the poet--

"The mansion's self was vast and venerable,
    With more of the monastic than has been
Elsewhere preserved; the cloisters still were stable,
    The cells, too, and refectory, I ween;
An exquisite small chapel had been able,
    Still unimpair'd, to decorate the scene;
The rest had been reformed, replaced, or sunk,
    And spoke more of the friar than the monk.

"Huge halls, long galleries, spacious chambers, joined
    By no quite lawful marriage of the arts,
Might shock a connoisseur; but when combined
    Formed a whole, which, irregular in parts,
Yet left a grand impression on the mind,
    At least of those whose eyes were in their hearts."

It is not my intention to lay open the scenes of domestic life at the Abbey, nor to describe the festivities of which I was a partaker during my sojourn within its hospitable walls. I wish merely to present a picture of the edifice itself, and of those personages and circumstances about it, connected with the memory of Byron.

I forbear, therefore, to dwell on my reception by my excellent and amiable host and hostess, or to make my reader acquainted with the elegant inmates of the mansion that I met in the saloon; and I shall pass on at once with him to the chamber allotted me, and to which I was most respectfully conducted by the chamberlain.

It was one of a magnificent suite of rooms, extending between the court of the cloisters and the Abbey garden, the windows looking into the latter. The whole suite formed the ancient state apartment, and had fallen into decay during the neglected days of the Abbey, so as to be in a ruinous condition in the time of Lord Byron. It had since been restored to its ancient splendor, of which my chamber may be cited as a specimen. It was lofty and well proportioned; the lower part of the walls was panelled with ancient oak, the upper part hung with gobelin tapestry, representing oriental hunting scenes, wherein the figures were of the size of life, and of great vivacity of attitude and color.

The furniture was antique, dignified, and cumbrous. High-backed chairs curiously carved, and wrought in needlework; a massive clothes-press of dark oak, well polished, and inlaid with landscapes of various tinted woods; a bed of state, ample and lofty, so as only to be ascended by a movable flight of steps, the huge posts supporting a high tester with a tuft of crimson plumes at each corner, and rich curtains of crimson damask hanging in broad and heavy folds.

A venerable mirror of plate glass stood on the toilet, in which belles of former centuries may have contemplated and decorated their charms. The floor of the chamber was of tesselated oak, shining with wax, and partly covered by a Turkey carpet. In the centre stood a massy oaken table, waxed and polished as smooth as glass, and furnished with a writing-desk of perfumed rosewood.

A sober light was admitted into the room through Gothic stone-shafted casements, partly shaded by crimson curtains, and partly overshadowed by the trees of the garden. This solemnly tempered light added to the effect of the stately and antiquated interior.

Two portraits, suspended over the doors, were in keeping with the scene. They were in ancient Vandyke dresses; one was a cavalier, who may have occupied this apartment in days of yore, the other was a lady with a black velvet mask in her hand, who may once have arrayed herself for conquest at the very mirror I have described.

The most curious relic of old times, however, in this quaint but richly dight apartment, was a great chimney-piece of panel-work, carved in high relief, with niches or compartments, each containing a human bust, that protruded almost entirely from the wall. Some of the figures were in ancient Gothic garb; the most striking among them was a female, who was earnestly regarded by a fierce Saracen from an adjoining niche.

This panel-work is among the mysteries of the Abbey, and causes as much wide speculation as the Egyptian hieroglyphics. Some suppose it to illustrate an adventure in the Holy Land, and that the lady in effigy had been rescued by some Crusader of the family from the turbaned Turk who watches her so earnestly. What tends to give weight to these suppositions is, that similar pieces of panel-work exist in other parts of the Abbey, in all of which are to be seen the Christian lady and her Saracen guardian or lover. At the bottom of these sculptures are emblazoned the armorial bearings of the Byrons.

I shall not detain the reader, however, with any further description of my apartment, or of the mysteries connected with it. As he is to pass some days with me at the Abbey, we shall have time to examine the old edifice at our leisure, and to make ourselves acquainted, not merely with its interior, but likewise with its environs.

THE ABBEY GARDEN.

The morning after my arrival, I rose at an early hour. The daylight was peering brightly between the window curtains, and drawing them apart, I gazed through the Gothic casement upon a scene that accorded in character with the interior of the ancient mansion. It was the old Abbey garden, but altered to suit the tastes of different times and occupants. In one direction were shady walls and alleys, broad terraces and lofty groves; in another, beneath a gray monastic-looking angle of the edifice, overrun with ivy and surmounted by a cross, lay a small French garden, with formal flower-pots, gravel walks, and stately stone balustrades.

The beauty of the morning, and the quiet of the hour, tempted me to an early stroll; for it is pleasant to enjoy such old-time places alone, when one may indulge poetical reveries, and spin cobweb fancies, without interruption. Dressing myself, therefore, with all speed, I descended a small flight of steps from the state apartment into the long corridor over the cloisters, along which I passed to a door at the farther end. Here I emerged into the open air, and, descending another flight of stone steps, found myself in the centre of what had once been the Abbey chapel.

Nothing of the sacred edifice remained, however, but the Gothic front, with its deep portal and grand lancet window, already described. The nave, the side walls, the choir, the sacristy, all had disappeared. The open sky was over my head, a smooth shaven grass-plot beneath my feet. Gravel walks and shrubberies had succeeded to the shadowy isles, and stately trees to the clustering columns.

"Where now the grass exhales a murky dew,
 The humid pall of life-extinguished clay,
 In sainted fame the sacred fathers grew,
 Nor raised their pious voices but to pray.
 Where now the bats their wavering wings extend,
 Soon as the gloaming spreads her warning shade,
 The choir did oft their mingling vespers blend,
 Or matin orisons to Mary paid."

Instead of the matin orisons of the monks, however, the ruined walls of the chapel now resounded to the cawing of innumerable rooks that were fluttering and hovering about the dark grove which they inhabited, and preparing for their morning flight.

My ramble led me along quiet alleys, bordered by shrubbery, where the solitary water-hen would now and then scud across my path, and take refuge among the bushes. From hence I entered upon a broad terraced walk, once a favorite resort of the friars, which extended the whole length of the old Abbey garden, passing along the ancient stone wall which bounded it. In the centre of the garden lay one of the monkish fish-pools, an oblong sheet of water, deep set like a mirror, in green sloping banks of turf. In its glassy bosom was reflected the dark mass of a neighboring grove, one of the most important features of the garden. This grove goes by the sinister name of "the Devil's Wood," and enjoys but an equivocal character in the neighborhood. It was planted by "The Wicked Lord Byron," during the early part of his residence at the Abbey, before his fatal duel with Mr. Chaworth. Having something of a foreign and classical taste, he set up leaden statues of satyrs or fauns at each end of the grove. The statues, like everything else about the old Lord, fell under the suspicion and obloquy that overshadowed him in the latter part of his life. The country people, who knew nothing of heathen mythology and its sylvan deities, looked with horror at idols invested with the diabolical attributes of horns and cloven feet. They probably supposed them some object of secret worship of the gloomy and secluded misanthrope and reputed murderer, and gave them the name of "The old Lord's Devils."

I penetrated the recesses of the mystic grove. There stood the ancient and much slandered statues, overshadowed by tall larches, and stained by dank green mold. It is not a matter of surprise that strange figures, thus behoofed and be-horned, and set up in a gloomy grove, should perplex the minds of the simple and superstitious yeomanry. There are many of the tastes and caprices of the rich, that in the eyes of the uneducated must savor of insanity.

I was attracted to this grove, however, by memorials of a more touching character. It had been one of the favorite haunts of the late Lord Byron. In his farewell visit to the Abbey, after he had parted with the possession of it, he passed some time in this grove, in company with his sister; and as a last memento, engraved their names on the bark of a tree.

The feelings that agitated his bosom during this farewell visit, when he beheld round him objects dear to his pride, and dear to his juvenile recollections, but of which the narrowness of his fortune would not permit him to retain possession, may be gathered from a passage in a poetical epistle, written to his sister in after years:

I did remind you of our own dear lake
  By the old hall, *which may be mine no more;*
Leman's is fair; but think not I forsake

The sweet remembrance of a dearer shore:
Sad havoc Time must with my memory make
  Ere *that* or *thou* can fade these eyes before;
Though, like all things which I have loved, they are
Resign'd for ever, or divided far.
I feel almost at times as I have felt
  In happy childhood; trees, and flowers, and brooks.
Which do remember me of where I dwelt
  Ere my young mind was sacrificed to books,
Come as of yore upon me, and can melt
  My heart with recognition, of their looks;
And even at moments I would think I see
Some living things I love--but none like thee."

I searched the grove for some time, before I found the tree on which
Lord Byron had left his frail memorial. It was an elm of peculiar form,
having two trunks, which sprang from the same root, and, after growing
side by side, mingled their branches together. He had selected it,
doubtless, as emblematical of his sister and himself. The names of
BYRON and AUGUSTA were still visible. They had been deeply cut in the
bark, but the natural growth of the tree was gradually rendering them
illegible, and a few years hence, strangers will seek in vain for this
record of fraternal affection.

Leaving the grove, I continued my ramble along a spacious terrace,
overlooking what had once been the kitchen garden of the Abbey. Below
me lay the monks' stew, or fish pond, a dark pool, overhung by gloomy
cypresses, with a solitary water-hen swimming about in it.

A little farther on, and the terrace looked down upon the stately scene
on the south side of the Abbey; the flower garden, with its stone
balustrades and stately peacocks, the lawn, with its pheasants and
partridges, and the soft valley of Newstead beyond.

At a distance, on the border of the lawn, stood another memento of Lord Byron; an oak planted by him in his boyhood, on his first visit to the Abbey. With a superstitious feeling inherent in him, he linked his own destiny with that of the tree. "As it fares," said he, "so will fare my fortunes." Several years elapsed, many of them passed in idleness and dissipation. He returned to the Abbey a youth scarce grown to manhood, but, as he thought, with vices and follies beyond his years. He found his emblem oak almost choked by weeds and brambles, and took the lesson to himself.

"Young oak, when I planted thee deep in the ground,
  I hoped that thy days would be longer than mine,
That thy dark waving branches would flourish around,
  And ivy thy trunk with its mantle entwine.

"Such, such was my hope--when in infancy's years
  On the laud of my fathers I reared thee with pride;
They are past, and I water thy stem with my tears--
Thy decay not the weeds that surround thee can hide."

I leaned over the stone balustrade of the terrace, and gazed upon the valley of Newstead, with its silver sheets of water gleaming in the morning sun. It was a sabbath morning, which always seems to have a hallowed influence over the landscape, probably from the quiet of the day, and the cessation of all kinds of week-day labor. As I mused upon the mild and beautiful scene, and the wayward destinies of the man, whose stormy temperament forced him from this tranquil paradise to battle with the passions and perils of the world, the sweet chime of bells from a village a few miles distant came stealing up the valley. Every sight and sound this morning seemed calculated to summon up touching recollections of poor Byron. The chime was from the village spire of Hucknall Torkard, beneath which his remains lie buried!

----I have since visited his tomb. It is in an old gray country church, venerable with the lapse of centuries. He lies buried beneath the pavement, at one end of the principal aisle. A light falls on the spot through the stained glass of a Gothic window, and a tablet on the adjacent wall announces the family vault of the Byrons. It had been the wayward intention of the poet to be entombed, with his faithful dog, in the monument erected by him in the garden of Newstead Abbey. His executors showed better judgment and feeling, in consigning his ashes to the family sepulchre, to mingle with those of his mother and his kindred. Here,

> "After life's fitful fever, he sleeps well.
> Malice domestic, foreign levy, nothing
> Can touch him further!"

How nearly did his dying hour realize the wish made by him, but a few years previously, in one of his fitful moods of melancholy and misanthropy:

> "When time, or soon or late, shall bring
>   The dreamless sleep that lulls the dead,
> Oblivion! may thy languid wing
>   Wave gently o'er my dying bed!
>
> "No band of friends or heirs be there,
>   To weep or wish the coining blow:
> No maiden with dishevelled hair,
>   To feel, or fein decorous woe.
>
> "But silent let me sink to earth.
>   With no officious mourners near:
> I would not mar one hour of mirth,

Nor startle friendship with a tear."

He died among strangers, in a foreign land, without a kindred hand to close his eyes; yet he did not die unwept. With all his faults and errors, and passions and caprices, he had the gift of attaching his humble dependents warmly to him. One of them, a poor Greek, accompanied his remains to England, and followed them to the grave. I am told that, during the ceremony, he stood holding on by a pew in an agony of grief, and when all was over, seemed as if he would have gone down into the tomb with the body of his master.--A nature that could inspire such attachments, must have been generous and beneficent.

PLOUGH MONDAY.

Sherwood Forest is a region that still retains much of the quaint customs and holiday games of the olden time. A day or two after my arrival at the Abbey, as I was walking in the cloisters, I heard the sound of rustic music, and now and then a burst of merriment, proceeding from the interior of the mansion. Presently the chamberlain came and informed me that a party of country lads were in the servants' hall, performing Plough Monday antics, and invited me to witness their mummery. I gladly assented, for I am somewhat curious about these relics of popular usages. The servants' hall was a fit place for the exhibition of an old Gothic game. It was a chamber of great extent, which in monkish times had been the refectory of the Abbey. A row of massive columns extended lengthwise through the centre, whence sprung Gothic arches, supporting the low vaulted ceiling. Here was a set of rustics dressed up in something of the style represented in the books concerning popular antiquities. One was in a rough garb of frieze, with his head muffled in bear-skin, and a bell dangling behind him, that jingled at every movement. He was the clown, or fool of the party, probably a traditional representative of the ancient satyr. The rest were decorated with ribbons and armed with wooden swords. The leader of the troop recited the old ballad of St. George and the Dragon, which had been current among the country people for ages; his companions accompanied the recitation with some rude attempt at acting, while the clown cut all kinds of antics.

To these succeeded a set of morris-dancers, gayly dressed up with ribbons and hawks'-bells. In this troop we had Robin Hood and Maid Marian, the latter represented by a smooth-faced boy; also Beelzebub, equipped with a broom, and accompanied by his wife Bessy, a termagant old beldame. These rude pageants are the lingering remains of the old customs of Plough Monday, when bands of rustics, fantastically dressed, and furnished with pipe and tabor, dragged what was called the "fool plough" from house to house, singing ballads and performing antics, for which they were rewarded with money and good cheer.

But it is not in "merry Sherwood Forest" alone that these remnants of old times prevail. They are to be met with in most of the counties north of the Trent, which classic stream seems to be the boundary line of primitive customs. During my recent Christmas sojourn at Barlboro' Hall, on the skirts of Derbyshire and Yorkshire, I had witnessed many of the rustic festivities peculiar to that joyous season, which have rashly been pronounced obsolete, by those who draw their experience merely from city life. I had seen the great Yule log put on the fire on Christmas Eve, and the wassail bowl sent round, brimming with its spicy beverage. I had heard carols beneath my window by the choristers of the neighboring village, who went their rounds about the ancient Hall at midnight, according to immemorial custom. We had mummers and mimers too, with the story of St. George and the Dragon, and other ballads and traditional dialogues, together with the famous old interlude of the

Hobby Horse, all represented in the antechamber and servants' hall by rustics, who inherited the custom and the poetry from preceding generations. The boar's head, crowned with rosemary, had taken its honored station among the Christmas cheer; the festal board had been attended by glee singers and minstrels from the village to entertain the company with hereditary songs and catches during their repast; and the old Pyrrhic game of the sword dance, handed down since the time of the Romans, was admirably performed in the court-yard of the mansion by a band of young men, lithe and supple in their forms and graceful in their movements, who, I was told, went the rounds of the villages and country-seats during the Christmas holidays.

I specify these rural pageants and ceremonials, which I saw during my sojourn in this neighborhood, because it has been deemed that some of the anecdotes of holiday customs given in my preceding writings, related to usages which have entirely passed away. Critics who reside in cities have little idea of the primitive manners and observances, which still prevail in remote and rural neighborhoods.

In fact, in crossing the Trent one seems to step back into old times; and in the villages of Sherwood Forest we are in a black-letter region. The moss-green cottages, the lowly mansions of gray stone, the Gothic crosses at each end of the villages, and the tall Maypole in the centre, transport us in imagination to foregone centuries; everything has a quaint and antiquated air.

The tenantry on the Abbey estate partake of this primitive character. Some of the families have rented farms there for nearly three hundred years; and, notwithstanding that their mansions fell to decay, and every thing about them partook of the general waste and misrule of the Byron dynasty, yet nothing could uproot them from their native soil. I am happy to say, that Colonel Wildman has taken these stanch loyal families under his peculiar care. He has favored them in their rents, repaired, or rather rebuilt their farm-houses, and has enabled families that had almost sunk into the class of mere rustic laborers, once more to hold up their heads among the yeomanry of the land.

I visited one of these renovated establishments that had but lately been a mere ruin, and now was a substantial grange. It was inhabited by a young couple. The good woman showed every part of the establishment with decent pride, exulting in its comfort and respectability. Her husband, I understood, had risen in consequence with the improvement of his mansion, and now began to be known among his rustic neighbors by the appellation of "the young Squire."

OLD SERVANTS.

In an old, time-worn, and mysterious looking mansion like Newstead Abbey, and one so haunted by monkish, and feudal, and poetical associations, it is a prize to meet with some ancient crone, who has passed a long life about the place, so as to have become a living chronicle of its fortunes and vicissitudes. Such a one is Nanny Smith, a worthy dame, near seventy years of age, who for a long time served as housekeeper to the Byrons, The Abbey and its domains comprise her world, beyond which she knows nothing, but within which she has ever conducted herself with native shrewdness and old-fashioned honesty. When Lord Byron sold the Abbey her vocation was at an end, still she lingered about the place, having for it the local attachment of a cat. Abandoning her comfortable housekeeper's apartment, she took shelter in one of the "rockhouses," which are nothing more than a little neighborhood of cabins, excavated in the perpendicular walls of a stone quarry, at no great distance from the Abbey. Three cells cut in the living rock, formed her dwelling; these she fitted up humbly but comfortably; her son William labored in the neighborhood, and aided to support her, and Nanny Smith maintained a cheerful aspect and an independent spirit. One of her gossips suggested to her that William should marry, and bring home a young wife to help her and take care of her. "Nay, nay," replied Nanny, tartly, "I want no young mistress in *my house*." So much for the love of rule--poor Nanny's house was a hole in a rock!

Colonel Wildman, on taking possession of the Abbey, found Nanny Smith thus humbly nestled. With that active benevolence which characterizes him, he immediately set William up in a small farm on the estate, where Nanny Smith has a comfortable mansion in her old days. Her pride is roused by her son's advancement. She remarks with exultation that people treat William with much more respect now that he is a farmer, than they did when he was a laborer. A farmer of the neighborhood has even endeavored to make a match between him and his sister, but Nanny Smith has grown fastidious, and interfered. The girl, she said, was too old for her son, besides, she did not see that he was in any need of a wife.

"No," said William, "I ha' no great mind to marry the wench: but if the Colonel and his lady wish it, I am willing. They have been so kind to me that I should think it my duty to please them." The Colonel and his lady, however, have not thought proper to put honest William's gratitude to so severe a test.

Another worthy whom Colonel Wildman found vegetating upon the place, and who had lived there for at least sixty years, was old Joe Murray. He had come there when a mere boy in the train of the "old lord," about the middle of the last century, and had continued with him until his death. Having been a cabin boy when very young, Joe always fancied himself a bit of a sailor; and had charge of all the pleasure-boats on the lake though he afterward rose to the dignity of butler. In the latter days of the old Lord Byron, when he shut himself up from all the world, Joe Murray was the only servant retained by him, excepting his housekeeper, Betty Hardstaff, who was reputed to have an undue sway over him, and was derisively called Lady Betty among the country folk.

When the Abbey came into the possession of the late Lord Byron, Joe Murray accompanied it as a fixture. He was reinstated as butler in the Abbey, and high admiral on the lake, and his sturdy honest mastiff qualities won so upon Lord Byron as even to rival his Newfoundland dog in his affections. Often when dining, he would pour out a bumper of choice Madeira, and hand it to Joe as he stood behind his chair. In fact, when he built the monumental tomb which stands in the Abbey garden, he intended it for himself, Joe Murray, and the dog. The two latter were to lie on each side of him. Boatswain died not long afterward, and was regularly interred, and the well-known epitaph inscribed on one side of the monument. Lord Byron departed for Greece; during his absence, a gentleman to whom Joe Murray was showing the tomb, observed, "Well, old boy, you will take your place here some twenty years hence."

"I don't know that, sir," growled Joe, in reply, "if I was sure his Lordship would come here, I should like it well enough, but I should not like to lie alone with the dog."

Joe Murray was always extremely neat in his dress, and attentive to his person, and made a most respectable appearance. A portrait of him still hangs in the Abbey, representing him a hale fresh-looking fellow, in a flaxen wig, a blue coat and buff waistcoat, with a pipe in his hand. He discharged all the duties of his station with great fidelity, unquestionable honesty, and much outward decorum, but, if we may believe his contemporary, Nanny Smith, who, as housekeeper, shared the sway of the household with him, he was very lax in his minor morals, and used to sing loose and profane songs as he presided at the table in the servants' hall, or sat taking his ale and smoking his pipe by the evening fire. Joe had evidently derived his convivial notions from the race of English country squires who flourished in the days of his juvenility. Nanny Smith was scandalized at his ribald songs, but being above harm herself, endured them in silence. At length, on his singing them before a young girl of sixteen, she could contain herself no longer, but read him a lecture that made his ears ring, and then flounced off to bed. The lecture seems, by her account, to have staggered Joe, for he told her the next morning that he had had a terrible dream in the night. An Evangelist stood at the foot of his bed with a great Dutch Bible, which he held with the printed part toward him, and after a while pushed it in his face. Nanny Smith undertook to interpret the vision, and read from it such a homily, and deduced such awful warnings, that Joe became quite serious, left off singing, and took to reading good books for a month; but after that, continued Nanny, he relapsed and became as bad as ever, and continued to sing loose and profane songs to his dying day.

When Colonel Wildman became proprietor of the Abbey he found Joe Murray flourishing in a green old age, though upward of fourscore, and continued him in his station as butler. The old man was rejoiced at the extensive repairs that were immediately commenced, and anticipated with pride the day when the Abbey should rise out of its ruins with renovated splendor, its gates be thronged with trains and equipages, and its halls once more echo to the sound of joyous hospitality.

What chiefly, however, concerned Joe's pride and ambition, was a plan of the Colonel's to have the ancient refectory of the convent, a great vaulted room, supported by Gothic columns, converted into a servants' hall. Here Joe looked forward to rule the roast at the head of the servants' table, and to make the Gothic arches ring with those hunting and hard-drinking ditties which were the horror of the discreet Nanny Smith. Time, however, was fast wearing away with him, and his great fear was that the hall would not be completed in his day. In his eagerness to hasten the repairs, he used to get up early in the morning, and ring up the workmen. Notwithstanding his great age, also, he would turn out half-dressed in cold weather to cut sticks for the fire. Colonel Wildman kindly remonstrated with him for thus risking his health, as others would do the work for him.

"Lord, sir," exclaimed the hale old fellow, "it's my air-bath, I'm all the better for it."

Unluckily, as he was thus employed one morning a splinter flew up and wounded one of his eyes. An inflammation took place; he lost the sight of that eye, and subsequently of the other. Poor Joe gradually pined away, and grew melancholy. Colonel Wildman kindly tried to cheer him up--"Come, come, old boy," cried he, "be of good heart, you will yet take your place in the servants' hall."

"Nay, nay, sir," replied he, "I did hope once that I should live to see it--I looked forward to it with pride, I confess, but it is all over with me now--I shall soon go home!" He died shortly afterward, at the advanced age of eighty-six, seventy of which had been passed as an honest and faithful servant at the Abbey. Colonel Wildman had him decently interred in the church of Hucknall Torkard, near the vault of Lord Byron.

SUPERSTITIONS OF THE ABBEY.

The anecdotes I had heard of the quondam housekeeper of Lord Byron, rendered me desirous of paying her a visit. I rode in company with Colonel Wildman, therefore, to the cottage of her son William, where she resides, and found her seated by her fireside, with a favorite cat perched upon her shoulder and purring in her ear. Nanny Smith is a large, good-looking woman, a specimen of the old-fashioned country housewife, combining antiquated notions and prejudices, and very limited information, with natural good sense. She loves to gossip about the Abbey and Lord Byron, and was soon drawn into a course of anecdotes, though mostly of an humble kind, such as suited the meridian of the housekeeper's room and servants' hall. She seemed to entertain a kind recollection of Lord Byron, though she had evidently been much perplexed by some of his vagaries; and especially by the means he adopted to counteract his tendency to corpulency. He used various modes to sweat himself down; sometimes he would lie for a long time in a warm bath, sometimes he would walk up the hills in the park, wrapped up and loaded with great coats; "a sad toil for the poor youth," added Nanny, "he being so lame."

His meals were scanty and irregular, consisting of dishes which Nanny seemed to hold in great contempt, such as pillau, macaroni, and light puddings.

She contradicted the report of the licentious life which he was reported to lead at the Abbey, and of the paramours said to have been brought with him from London. "A great part of his time used to be passed lying on a sofa reading. Sometimes he had young gentlemen of his acquaintance with him, and they played some mad pranks; but nothing but what young gentlemen may do, and no harm done."

"Once, it is true," she added, "he had with him a beautiful boy as a page, which the housemaids said was a girl. For my part, I know nothing about it. Poor soul, he was so lame he could not go out much with the men; all the comfort he had was to be a little with the lasses. The housemaids, however, were very jealous; one of them, in particular, took the matter in great dudgeon. Her name was Lucy; she was a great favorite with Lord Byron, and had been much noticed by him, and began to have high notions. She had her fortune told by a man who squinted, to whom she gave two-and-sixpence. He told her to hold up her head and look high, for she would come to great things. Upon this," added Nanny, "the poor thing dreamt of nothing less than becoming a lady, and mistress of the Abbey; and promised me, if such luck should happen to her, she would be a good friend to me. Ah well-a-day! Lucy never had the fine fortune she dreamt of; but she had better than I thought for; she is now married, and keeps a public house at Warwick."

Finding that we listened to her with great attention, Nanny Smith went on with her gossiping. "One time," said she, "Lord Byron took a notion that there was a deal of money buried about the Abbey by the monks in old times, and nothing would serve him but he must have the flagging taken up in the cloisters; and they digged and digged, but found nothing but stone coffins full of bones. Then he must needs have one of the coffins put in one end of the great hall, so that the servants were afraid to go there of nights. Several of the skulls were cleaned and put in frames in his room. I used to have to go into the room at night to shut the windows, and if I glanced an eye at them, they all seemed to grin; which I believe skulls always do. I can't say but I was glad to get out of the room.

"There was at one time (and for that matter there is still) a good deal said about ghosts haunting about the Abbey. The keeper's wife said she saw two standing in a dark part of the cloisters just opposite the chapel, and one in the garden by the lord's well. Then there was a young lady, a cousin of Lord Byron, who was staying in the Abbey and slept in the room next the clock; and she told me that one night when she was lying in bed, she saw a lady in white come out of the wall on one side of the room, and go into the wall on the opposite side.

"Lord Byron one day said to me, 'Nanny, what nonsense they tell about ghosts, as if there ever were any such things. I have never seen any thing of the kind about the Abbey, and I warrant you have not.' This was all done, do you see, to draw me out; but I said nothing, but shook my head. However, they say his lordship did once see something. It was in the great hall--something all black and hairy, he said it was the devil.

"For my part," continued Nanny Smith, "I never saw anything of the kind--but I heard something once. I was one evening scrubbing the floor of the little dining-room at the end of the long gallery; it was after dark; I expected every moment to be called to tea, but wished to finish what I was about. All at once I heard heavy footsteps in the great hall. They sounded like the tramp of a horse. I took the light and went to see what it was. I heard the steps come from the lower end of the hall to the fireplace in the centre, where they stopped; but I could see nothing. I returned to my work, and in a little time heard the same noise again. I went again with the light; the footsteps stopped by the fireplace as before; still I could see nothing. I returned to my work, when I heard the steps for a third time. I then went into the hall without a light, but they stopped just the same, by the fireplace, half way up the hall. I thought this rather odd, but returned to my work. When it was finished, I took the light and went through the hall, as that was my way to the kitchen. I heard no more footsteps, and thought no more of the matter, when, on coming to the lower end of the hall, I found the door locked, and then, on one side of the door, I saw the stone coffin with the skull and bones that had been digged up in the cloisters."

Here Nanny paused. I asked her if she believed that the mysterious footsteps had any connection with the skeleton in the coffin; but she shook her head, and would not commit herself. We took our leave of the good old dame shortly after, and the story she had related gave subject for conversation on our ride homeward. It was evident she had spoken the truth as to what she had heard, but had been deceived by some peculiar effect of sound. Noises are propagated about a huge irregular edifice of the kind in a very deceptive manner; footsteps are prolonged and reverberated by the vaulted cloisters and echoing halls; the creaking and slamming of distant gates, the rushing of the blast through the groves and among the ruined arches of the chapel, have all a strangely delusive effect at night. Colonel Wildman gave an instance of the kind from his own experience. Not long after he had taken up his residence at the Abbey, he heard one moonlight night a noise as if a carriage was passing at a distance. He opened the window and leaned out. It then seemed as if the great iron roller was dragged along the gravel walks and terrace, but there was nothing to be seen. When he saw the gardener on the following morning, he questioned him about working so late at night. The gardener declared that no one had been at work, and the roller was chained up. He was sent to examine it, and came back with a countenance full of surprise. The roller had been moved in the night, but he declared no mortal hand could have moved it. "Well," replied the Colonel, good-humoredly, "I am glad to find I have a brownie to work for me."

Lord Byron did much to foster and give currency to the superstitious tales connected with the Abbey, by believing, or pretending to believe in them. Many have supposed that his mind was really tinged with superstition, and that this innate infirmity was increased by passing much of his time in a lonely way, about the empty halls and cloisters of the Abbey, then in a ruinous melancholy state, and brooding over the skulls and effigies of its former inmates. I should rather think that he found poetical enjoyment in these supernatural themes, and that his imagination delighted to people this gloomy and romantic pile with all kinds of shadowy inhabitants. Certain it is, the aspect of the mansion under the varying influence of twilight and moonlight, and cloud and sunshine operating upon its halls, and galleries, and monkish cloisters, is enough to breed all kinds of fancies in the minds of its inmates, especially if poetically or superstitiously inclined.

I have already mentioned some of the fabled visitants of the Abbey. The goblin friar, however, is the one to whom Lord Byron has given the greatest importance. It walked the cloisters by night, and sometimes glimpses of it were seen in other parts of the Abbey. Its appearance was said to portend some impending evil to the master of the mansion. Lord Byron pretended to have seen it about a month before he contracted his ill-starred marriage with Miss Milbanke.

He has embodied this tradition in the following ballad, in which he represents the friar as one of the ancient inmates of the Abbey, maintaining by night a kind of spectral possession of it, in right of the fraternity. Other traditions, however, represent him as one of the friars doomed to wander about the place in atonement for his crimes. But to the ballad--

"Beware! beware! of the Black Friar,
  Who sitteth by Norman stone,
For he mutters his prayers in the midnight air,
  And his mass of the days that are gone.
When the Lord of the Hill, Amundeville,
  Made Norman Church his prey,
And expell'd the friars, one friar still
  Would not be driven away.

"Though he came in his might, with King Henry's right,
  To turn church lands to lay,
With sword in hand, and torch to light
  Their walls, if they said nay,
A monk remain'd, unchased, unchain'd,
  And he did not seem form'd of clay,
For he's seen in the porch, and he's seen in the church,
  Though he is not seen by day.

"And whether for good, or whether for ill,
  It is not mine to say;
But still to the house of Amundeville
  He abideth night and day.
By the marriage bed of their lords, 'tis said,
  He flits on the bridal eve;
And 'tis held as faith, to their bed of death,
  He comes--but not to grieve.

"When an heir is born, he is heard to mourn,
  And when aught is to befall
That ancient line, in the pale moonshine
  He walks from hall to hall.
His form you may trace, but not his face,
  'Tis shadow'd by his cowl;
But his eyes may be seen from the folds between,
  And they seem of a parted soul.

"But beware! beware of the Black Friar,
  He still retains his sway,
For he is yet the church's heir,
  Whoever may be the lay.
Amundeville is lord by day,

> But the monk is lord by night,
> Nor wine nor wassail could raise a vassal
> To question that friar's right.
>
> "Say nought to him as he walks the hall,
>   And he'll say nought to you;
> He sweeps along in his dusky pall,
>   As o'er the grass the dew.
> Then gramercy! for the Black Friar;
>   Heaven sain him! fair or foul,
> And whatsoe'er may be his prayer
>   Let ours be for his soul."

Such is the story of the goblin friar, which, partly through old tradition, and partly through the influence of Lord Byron's rhymes, has become completely established in the Abbey, and threatens to hold possession so long as the old edifice shall endure. Various visitors have either fancied, or pretended to have seen him, and a cousin of Lord Byron, Miss Sally Parkins, is even said to have made a sketch of him from memory. As to the servants at the Abbey, they have become possessed with all kinds of superstitious fancies. The long corridors and Gothic halls, with their ancient portraits and dark figures in armor, are all haunted regions to them; they even fear to sleep alone, and will scarce venture at night on any distant errand about the Abbey unless they go in couples.

Even the magnificent chamber in which I was lodged was subject to the supernatural influences which reigned over the Abbey, and was said to be haunted by "Sir John Byron the Little with the great Beard." The ancient black-looking portrait of this family worthy, which hangs over the door of the great saloon, was said to descend occasionally at midnight from the frame, and walk the rounds of the state apartments. Nay, his visitations were not confined to the night, for a young lady, on a visit to the Abbey some years since, declared that, on passing in broad day by the door of the identical chamber I have described, which stood partly open, she saw Sir John Byron the Little seated by the fireplace, reading out of a great black-letter book. From this circumstance some have been led to suppose that the story of Sir John Byron may be in some measure connected with the mysterious sculptures of the chimney-piece already mentioned; but this has no countenance from the most authentic antiquarians of the Abbey.

For my own part, the moment I learned the wonderful stories and strange suppositions connected with my apartment, it became an imaginary realm to me. As I lay in bed at night and gazed at the mysterious panel-work, where Gothic knight, and Christian dame, and Paynim lover gazed upon me in effigy, I used to weave a thousand fancies concerning them. The great figures in the tapestry, also, were almost animated by the workings of my imagination, and the Vandyke portraits of the cavalier and lady that looked down with pale aspects from the wall, had almost a spectral effect, from their immovable gaze and silent companionship--

"For by dim lights the portraits of the dead
  Have something ghastly, desolate, and dread.
----Their buried looks still wave
  Along the canvas; their eyes glance like dreams
On ours, as spars within some dusky cave,
  But death is mingled in their shadowy beams."

In this way I used to conjure up fictions of the brain, and clothe the objects around me with ideal interest and import, until, as the Abbey clock tolled midnight, I almost looked to see Sir John Byron the Little with the long beard stalk into the room with his book under his arm, and take his seat beside the mysterious chimney-piece.

ANNESLEY HALL.

At about three miles' distance from Newstead Abbey, and contiguous to its lands, is situated Annesley Hall, the old family mansion of the Chaworths. The families, like the estates, of the Byrons and Chaworths, were connected in former times, until the fatal duel between their two representatives. The feud, however, which prevailed for a time, promised to be cancelled by the attachment of two youthful hearts. While Lord Byron was yet a boy, he beheld Mary Ann Chaworth, a beautiful girl, and the sole heiress of Annesley. With that susceptibility to female charms, which he evinced almost from childhood, he became almost immediately enamored of her. According to one of his biographers, it would appear that at first their attachment was mutual, yet clandestine. The father of Miss Chaworth was then living, and may have retained somewhat of the family hostility, for we are told that the interviews of Lord Byron and the young lady were private, at a gate which opened from her father's grounds to those of Newstead. However, they were so young at the time that these meetings could not have been regarded as of any importance: they were little more than children in years; but, as Lord Byron says of himself, his feelings were beyond his age.

The passion thus early conceived was blown into a flame, during a six weeks' vacation which he passed with his mother at Nottingham. The father of Miss Chaworth was dead, and she resided with her mother at the old Hall of Annesley. During Byron's minority, the estate of Newstead was let to Lord Grey de Ruthen, but its youthful Lord was always a welcome guest at the Abbey. He would pass days at a time there, and make frequent visits thence to Annesley Hall. His visits were encouraged by Miss Chaworth's mother; she partook of none of the family feud, and probably looked with complacency upon an attachment that might heal old differences and unite two neighboring estates.

The six weeks' vacation passed as a dream amongst the beautiful flowers of Annesley. Byron was scarce fifteen years of age, Mary Chaworth was two years older; but his heart, as I have said, was beyond his age, and his tenderness for her was deep and passionate. These early loves, like the first run of the uncrushed grape, are the sweetest and strongest gushings of the heart, and however they may be superseded by other attachments in after years, the memory will continually recur to them, and fondly dwell upon their recollections.

His love for Miss Chaworth, to use Lord Byron's own expression, was "the romance of the most romantic period of his life," and I think we can trace the effect of it throughout the whole course of his writings, coming up every now and then, like some lurking theme which runs through a complicated piece of music, and links it all in a pervading chain of melody.

How tenderly and mournfully does he recall, in after years, the feelings awakened in his youthful and inexperienced bosom by this impassioned, yet innocent attachment; feelings, he says, lost or hardened in the intercourse of life:

"The love of better things and better days;
  The unbounded hope, and heavenly ignorance
Of what is called the world, and the world's ways;
  The moments when we gather from a glance
More joy than from all future pride or praise,
  Which kindle manhood, but can ne'er entrance
The heart in an existence of its own,
Of which another's bosom is the zone."

Whether this love was really responded to by the object, is uncertain. Byron sometimes speaks as if he had met with kindness in return, at other times lie acknowledges that she never gave 'him reason to believe she loved him. It is probable, however, that at first she experienced some flutterings of the heart. She was of a susceptible age; had as yet formed no other attachments; her lover, though boyish in years, was a man in intellect, a poet in imagination, and had a countenance of remarkable beauty.

With the six weeks' vacation ended this brief romance. Byron returned to school deeply enamored, but if he had really made any impression on Miss Chaworth's heart, it was too slight to stand the test of absence. She was at that age when a female soon changes from the girl to a woman, and leaves her boyish lovers far behind her. While Byron was pursuing his school-boy studies, she was mingling with society, and met with a gentleman of the name of Musters, remarkable, it is said, for manly beauty. A story is told of her having first seen him from the top of Annesley Hall, as he dashed through the park, with hound and horn, taking the lead of the whole field in a fox chase, and that she was struck by the spirit of his appearance, and his admirable horsemanship. Under such favorable auspices, he wooed and won her, and when Lord Byron next met her, he learned to his dismay that she was the affianced bride of another.

With that pride of spirit--which always distinguished him, he controlled his feelings and maintained a serene countenance. He even affected to speak calmly on the subject of her approaching nuptials. "The next time I see you," said he, "I suppose you will be Mrs. Chaworth" (for she was to retain her family name). Her reply was, "I hope so."

I have given these brief details preparatory to a sketch of a visit which I made to the scene of this youthful romance. Annesley Hall I understood was shut up, neglected, and almost in a state of desolation; for Mr. Musters rarely visited it, residing with his family in the neighborhood of Nottingham. I set out for the Hall on horseback, in company with Colonel Wildman, and followed by the great Newfoundland dog Boatswain. In the course of our ride we visited a spot memorable in the love story I have cited. It was the scene of this parting interview between Byron and Miss Chaworth, prior to her marriage. A long ridge of upland advances into the valley of Newstead, like a promontory into a lake, and was formerly crowned by a beautiful grove, a landmark to the neighboring country. The grove and promontory are graphically described by Lord Byron in his "Dream," and an exquisite picture given of himself, and the lovely object of his boyish idolatry--

"I saw two beings to the hues of youth
Standing upon a hill, a gentle hill,
Green, and of mild declivity, the last
As 'twere the cape of a long ridge of such,
Save that there was no sea to lave its base,
But a most living landscape, and the ware
Of woods and cornfields, and the abodes of men.
Scattered at intervals and wreathing smoke
Arising from such rustic roofs;--the hill
Was crown'd with a peculiar diadem
Of trees, in circular array, so fixed,
Not by the sport of nature, but of man:
These two, a maiden and a youth, were there
Gazing--the one on all that was beneath
Fair as herself--but the boy gazed on her;
And both were fair, and one was beautiful:
And both were young--yet not alike in youth:
As the sweet moon in the horizon's verge,
The maid was on the verge of womanhood;
The boy had fewer summers, but his heart

Had far outgrown his years, and to his eye
There was but one beloved face on earth,
And that was shining on him."

I stood upon the spot consecrated by this memorable interview. Below me
extended the "living landscape," once contemplated by the loving pair;
the gentle valley of Newstead, diversified by woods and corn-fields,
and village spires, and gleams of water, and the distant towers and
pinnacles of the venerable Abbey. The diadem of trees, however, was
gone. The attention drawn to it by the poet, and the romantic manner in
which he had associated it with his early passion for Mary Chaworth,
had nettled the irritable feelings of her husband, who but ill brooked
the poetic celebrity conferred on his wife by the enamored verses of
another. The celebrated grove stood on his estate, and in a fit of
spleen he ordered it to be levelled with the dust. At the time of my
visit the mere roots of the trees were visible; but the hand that laid
them low is execrated by every poetical pilgrim.

Descending the bill, we soon entered a part of what once was Annesley
Park, and rode among time-worn and tempest-riven oaks and elms, with
ivy clambering about their trunks, and rooks' nests among their
branches. The park had been cut up by a post-road, crossing which, we
came to the gate-house of Annesley Hall. It was an old brick building
that might have served as an outpost or barbacan to the Hall during the
civil wars, when every gentleman's house was liable to become a
fortress. Loopholes were still visible in its walls, but the peaceful
ivy had mantled the sides, overrun the roof, and almost buried the
ancient clock in front, that still marked the waning hours of its
decay.

An arched way led through the centre of the gate-house, secured by
grated doors of open iron work, wrought into flowers and flourishes.
These being thrown open, we entered a paved court-yard, decorated with

shrubs and antique flowerpots, with a ruined stone fountain in the centre. The whole approach resembled that of an old French chateau.

On one side of the court-yard was a range of stables, now tenantless, but which bore traces of the fox-hunting squire; for there were stalls boxed up, into which the hunters might be turned loose when they came home from the chase.

At the lower end of the court, and immediately opposite the gate-house, extended the Hall itself; a rambling, irregular pile, patched and pieced at various times, and in various tastes, with gable ends, stone balustrades, and enormous chimneys, that strutted out like buttresses from the walls. The whole front of the edifice was overrun with evergreens.

We applied for admission at the front door, which was under a heavy porch. The portal was strongly barricaded, and our knocking was echoed by waste and empty halls. Every thing bore an appearance of abandonment. After a time, however, our knocking summoned a solitary tenant from some remote corner of the pile. It was a decent-looking little dame, who emerged from a side door at a distance, and seemed a worthy inmate of the antiquated mansion. She had, in fact, grown old with it. Her name, she said, was Nanny Marsden; if she lived until next August, she would be seventy-one; a great part of her life had been passed in the Hall, and when the family had removed to Nottingham, she had been left in charge of it. The front of the house had been thus warily barricaded in consequence of the late riots at Nottingham, in the course of which the dwelling of her master had been sacked by the mob. To guard against any attempt of the kind upon the Hall, she had put it in this state of defence; though I rather think she and a superannuated gardener comprised the whole garrison. "You must be attached to the old building," said I, "after having lived so long in it." "Ah, sir!" replied she, "I am *getting in years*, and have a furnished cottage of my own in Annesley Wood, and begin to feel as if I should like to go and live in my own home."

Guided by the worthy little custodian of the fortress, we entered through the sally port by which she had issued forth, and soon found ourselves in a spacious, but somewhat gloomy hall, where the light was partially admitted through square stone-shafted windows, overhung with ivy. Everything around us had the air of an old-fashioned country squire's establishment. In the centre of the hall was a billiard-table, find about the walls were hung portraits of race-horses, hunters, and favorite dogs, mingled indiscriminately with family pictures.

Staircases led up from the hall to various apartments. In one of the rooms we were shown a couple of buff jerkins, and a pair of ancient jackboots, of the time of the cavaliers; relics which are often to be met with in the old English family mansions. These, however, had peculiar value, for the good little dame assured us that they had belonged to Robin Hood. As we were in the midst of the region over which that famous outlaw once bore ruffian sway, it was not for us to gainsay his claim to any of these venerable relics, though we might have demurred that the articles of dress here shown were of a date much later than his time. Every antiquity, however, about Sherwood Forest is apt to be linked with the memory of Robin Hood and his gang.

As we were strolling about the mansion, our four-footed attendant, Boatswain, followed leisurely, as if taking a survey of the premises. I turned to rebuke him for his intrusion, but the moment the old housekeeper understood he had belonged to Lord Byron, her heart seemed to yearn toward him. "Nay, nay," exclaimed she, "let him alone, let him go where he pleases. He's welcome. Ah, dear me! If he lived here I should take great care of him--he should want for nothing.--Well!" continued she, fondling him, "who would have thought that I should see a dog of Lord Byron in Annesley Hall!"

"I suppose, then," said I, "you recollect something of Lord Byron, when he used to visit here?" "Ah, bless him!" cried she, "that I do! He used to ride over here and stay three days at a time, and sleep in the blue room. Ah! poor fellow! He was very much taken with my young mistress; he used to walk about the garden and the terraces with her, and seemed to love the very ground she trod on. He used to call her his bright morning star of Annesley."

I felt the beautiful poetic phrase thrill through me.

"You appear to like the memory of Lord Byron," said I.

"Ah, sir! why should not I! He was always main good to me when he came here. Well, well, they say it is a pity he and my young lady did not make a match. Her mother would have liked it. He was always a welcome guest, and some think it would have been well for him to have had her; but it was not to be! He went away to school, and then Mr. Musters saw her, and so things took their course."

The simple soul now showed us into the favorite sitting-room of Miss Chaworth, with a small flower-garden under the windows, in which she had delighted. In this room Byron used to sit and listen to her as she played and sang, gazing upon her with the passionate, and almost painful devotion of a love-sick stripling. He himself gives us a glowing picture of his mute idolatry:

"He bad no breath, no being, but in hers;
She was his voice; he did not speak to her,
But trembled on her words; she was his sight.
For his eye followed hers, and saw with hers,
Which colored all his objects; he had ceased
To live within himself; she was his life,

The ocean to the river of his thoughts,
Which terminated all; upon a tone,
A touch of hers, his blood would ebb and flow,
And his cheek change tempestuously--his heart
Unknowing of its cause of agony."

There was a little Welsh air, call "Mary Ann," which, from bearing her own name, he associated with herself, and often persuaded her to sing it over and over for him.

The chamber, like all the other parts of the house, had a look of sadness and neglect; the flower-pots beneath the window, which once bloomed beneath the hand of Mary Chaworth, were overrun with weeds; and the piano, which had once vibrated to her touch, and thrilled the heart of her stripling lover, was now unstrung and out of tune.

We continued our stroll about the waste apartments, of all shapes and sizes, and without much elegance of decoration. Some of them were hung with family portraits, among which was pointed out that of the Mr. Chaworth who was killed by the "wicked Lord Byron."

These dismal looking portraits had a powerful effect upon the imagination of the stripling poet, on his first visit to the hall. As they gazed down from the wall, he thought they scowled upon him, as if they had taken a grudge against him on account of the duel of his ancestor. He even gave this as a reason, though probably in jest, for not sleeping at the Hall, declaring that he feared they would come down from their frames at night to haunt him.

A feeling of the kind he has embodied in one of his stanzas of "Don Juan:"

  "The forms of the grim knights and pictured saints

Look living in the moon; and as you turn
Backward and forward to the echoes faint
  Of your own footsteps--voices from the urn
Appear to wake, and shadows wild and quaint
  Start from the frames which fence their aspects stern,
As if to ask you how you dare to keep
A vigil there, where all but death should sleep."

Nor was the youthful poet singular in these fancies; the Hall, like
most old English mansions that have ancient family portraits hanging
about their dusky galleries and waste apartments, had its ghost story
connected with these pale memorials of the dead. Our simple-hearted
conductor stopped before the portrait of a lady, who had been a beauty
in her time, and inhabited the hall in the heyday of her charms.
Something mysterious or melancholy was connected with her story; she
died young, but continued for a long time to haunt the ancient mansion,
to the great dismay of the servants, and the occasional disquiet of the
visitors, and it was with much difficulty her troubled spirit was
conjured down and put to rest.

From the rear of the hall we walked out into the garden, about which
Byron used to stroll and loiter in company with Miss Chaworth. It was
laid out in the old French style. There was a long terraced walk, with
heavy stone balustrades and sculptured urns, overrun with ivy and
evergreens. A neglected shrubbery bordered one side of the terrace,
with a lofty grove inhabited by a venerable community of rooks. Great
flights of steps led down from the terrace to a flower garden laid out
in formal plots. The rear of the Hall, which overlooked the garden, had
the weather stains of centuries, and its stone-shafted casements and an
ancient sun-dial against its walls carried back the mind to days of
yore.

The retired and quiet garden, once a little sequestered world of love

and romance, was now all matted and wild, yet was beautiful, even in
its decay. Its air of neglect and desolation was in unison with the
fortune of the two beings who had once walked here in the freshness of
youth, and life, and beauty. The garden, like their young hearts, had
gone to waste and ruin.

Returning to the Hall we now visited a chamber built over the porch, or
grand entrance. It was in a ruinous condition, the ceiling having
fallen in and the floor given way. This, however, is a chamber rendered
interesting by poetical associations. It is supposed to be the oratory
alluded to by Lord Byron in his "Dream," wherein he pictures his
departure from Annesley, after learning that Mary Chaworth was engaged
to be married--

'There was an ancient mansion, and before
Its walls there was a steed caparisoned;
Within an antique oratory stood
The boy of whom I spake;--he was alone,
And pale and pacing to and fro: anon
He sate him down, and seized a pen, and traced
Words which I could not guess of; then he leaned
His bow'd head on his hands, and shook as 'twere
With a convulsion--then arose again,
And with his teeth and quivering hands did tear
What he had written, but he shed no tears.
And he did calm himself, and fix his brow
Into a kind of quiet; as he paused,
The lady of his love re-entered there;
She was serene and smiling then, and yet
She knew she was by him beloved,--she knew,
For quickly comes such knowledge, that his heart
Was darkened with her shadow, and she saw
That he was wretched, but she saw not all.

He rose, and with a cold and gentle grasp
He took her hand; a moment o'er his face
A tablet of unutterable thoughts
Was traced, and then it faded as it came;
He dropp'd the hand he held, and with slow steps
Return'd, but not as bidding her adieu,
For they did part with mutual smiles:--he pass'd
From out the massy gate of that old Hall,
And mounting on his steed he went his way,
And ne'er repassed that hoary threshold more."

In one of his journals, Lord Byron describes his feelings after thus leaving the oratory. Arriving on the summit of a hill, which commanded the last view of Annesley, he checked his horse, and gazed back with mingled pain and fondness upon the groves which embowered the Hall, and thought upon the lovely being that dwelt there, until his feelings were quite dissolved in tenderness. The conviction at length recurred that she never could be his, when, rousing himself from his reverie, he struck his spurs into his steed and dashed forward, as if by rapid motion to leave reflection behind him.

Yet, notwithstanding what he asserts in the verses last quoted, he did pass the "hoary threshold" of Annesley again. It was, however, after the lapse of several years, during which he had grown up to manhood, and had passed through the ordeal of pleasures and tumultuous passions, and had felt the influence of other charms. Miss Chaworth, too, had become a wife and a mother, and he dined at Annesley Hall at the invitation of her husband. He thus met the object of his early idolatry in the very scene of his tender devotions, which, as he says, her smiles had once made a heaven to him. The scene was but little changed. He was in the very chamber where he had so often listened entranced to the witchery of her voice; there were the same instruments and music; there lay her flower garden beneath the window, and the walks through which he had wandered with her in the intoxication of youthful love. Can we wonder that amidst the tender recollections which every object around him was calculated to awaken, the fond passion of his boyhood should rush back in full current to his heart? He was himself surprised at this sudden revulsion of his feelings, but he had acquired self-possession and could command them. His firmness, however, was doomed to undergo a further trial. While seated by the object of his secret devotions, with all these recollections throbbing in his bosom, her infant daughter was brought into the room. At sight of the child he started; it dispelled the last lingerings of his dream, and he afterward confessed, that to repress his emotion at the moment, was the severest part of his task.

The conflict of feelings that raged within his bosom, throughout this fond and tender, yet painful and embarrassing visit, are touchingly depicted in lines which he wrote immediately afterward, and which, though not addressed to her by name, are evidently intended for the eye and the heart of the fair lady of Annesley:

"Well! thou art happy, and I feel
  That I should thus be happy too;
For still my heart regards thy weal
  Warmly, as it was wont to do.

Thy husband's blest--and 'twill impart
  Some pangs to view his happier lot:
But let them pass--Oh! how my heart
  Would hate him, if he loved thee not!

"When late I saw thy favorite child
  I thought my jealous heart would break;
But when the unconscious infant smiled,
  I kiss'd it for its mother's sake.

"I kiss'd it, and repress'd my sighs
  Its father in its face to see;
But then it had its mother's eyes,
  And they were all to love and me.

"Mary, adieu! I must away:
  While thou art blest I'll not repine;
But near thee I can never stay:
  My heart would soon again be thine.

"I deem'd that time, I deem'd that pride
  Had quench'd at length my boyish flame
Nor knew, till seated by thy side,
  My heart in all, save love, the same.

"Yet I was calm: I knew the time
  My breast would thrill before thy look;
But now to tremble were a crime--
  We met, and not a nerve was shook.

"I saw thee gaze upon my face,
  Yet meet with no confusion there:
One only feeling could'st thou trace;
  The sullen calmness of despair.

"Away! away! my early dream
  Remembrance never must awake:
Oh! where is Lethe's fabled stream?
  My foolish heart, be still, or break."

The revival of this early passion, and the melancholy associations
which it spread over those scenes in the neighborhood of Newstead,

which would necessarily be the places of his frequent resort while in England, are alluded to by him as a principal cause of his first departure for the Continent:

"When man expell'd from Eden's bowers
  A moment lingered near the gate,
Each scene recalled the vanish'd hours,
  And bade him curse his future fate.

"But wandering on through distant climes,
  He learnt to bear his load of grief;
Just gave a sigh to other times,
  And found in busier scenes relief.

"Thus, Mary, must it be with me,
  And I must view thy charms no more;
For, while I linger near to thee,
  I sigh for all I knew before."

It was in the subsequent June that he set off on his pilgrimage by sea and land, which was to become the theme of his immortal poem. That the image of Mary Chaworth, as he saw and loved her in the days of his boyhood, followed him to the very shore, is shown in the glowing stanzas addressed to her on the eve of embarkation--

"'Tis done--and shivering in the gale
  The bark unfurls her snowy sail;
And whistling o'er the bending mast,
  Loud sings on high the fresh'ning blast;
And I must from this land be gone.
  Because I cannot love but one.

"And I will cross the whitening foam,

And I will seek a foreign home;
Till I forget a false fair face,
　I ne'er shall find a resting place;
My own dark thoughts I cannot shun,
　But ever love, and love but one.

"To think of every early scene,
　Of what we are, and what we've been,
Would whelm some softer hearts with woe--
　But mine, alas! has stood the blow;
Yet still beats on as it begun,
　And never truly loves but one.

"And who that dear loved one may be
　Is not for vulgar eyes to see,
And why that early love was cross'd,
　Thou know'st the best, I feel the most;
But few that dwell beneath the sun
　Have loved so long, and loved but one.

"I've tried another's fetters too,
　With charms, perchance, as fair to view;
And I would fain have loved as well,
　But some unconquerable spell
Forbade my bleeding breast to own
　A kindred care for aught but one.

"'Twould soothe to take one lingering view,
　And bless thee in my last adieu;
Yet wish I not those eyes to weep
　For him who wanders o'er the deep;
His home, his hope, his youth are gone,
　Yet still he loves, and loves but one."

The painful interview at Annesley Hall, which revived with such intenseness his early passion, remained stamped upon his memory with singular force, and seems to have survived all his "wandering through distant climes," to which he trusted as an oblivious antidote. Upward of two years after that event, when, having made his famous pilgrimage, he was once more an inmate of Newstead Abbey, his vicinity to Annesley Hall brought the whole scene vividly before him, and he thus recalls it in a poetic epistle to a friend--

"I've seen my bride another's bride,--
Have seen her seated by his side,--
Have seen the infant which she bore,
Wear the sweet smile the mother wore,
When she and I in youth have smiled
As fond and faultless as her child:--
Have seen her eyes, in cold disdain,
Ask if I felt no secret pain.

"And I have acted well my part,
And made my cheek belie my heart,
Returned the freezing glance she gave,
Yet felt the while *that* woman's slave;--
Have kiss'd, as if without design,
The babe which ought to have been mine,
And show'd, alas! in each caress,
Time had not made me love the less."

"It was about the time," says Moore in his life of Lord Byron, "when he was thus bitterly feeling and expressing the blight which his heart had suffered from a **real** object of affection, that his poems on an imaginary one, 'Thyrza,' were written." He was at the same time grieving over the loss of several of his earliest and dearest friends the companions of his joyous school-boy hours. To recur to the beautiful language of Moore, who writes with the kindred and kindling sympathies of a true poet: "All these recollections of the young and the dead mingled themselves in his mind with the image of her, who, though living, was for him, as much lost as they, and diffused that general feeling of sadness and fondness through his soul, which found a vent in these poems.... It was the blending of the two affections in his memory and imagination, that gave birth to an ideal object combining the best features of both, and drew from him those saddest and tenderest of love poems, in which we find all the depth and intensity of real feeling, touched over with such a light as no reality ever wore."

An early, innocent, and unfortunate passion, however fruitful of pain it may be to the man, is a lasting advantage to the poet. It is a well of sweet and bitter fancies; of refined and gentle sentiments; of elevated and ennobling thoughts; shut up in the deep recesses of the heart, keeping it green amidst the withering blights of the world, and, by its casual gushings and overflowings, recalling at times all the freshness, and innocence, and enthusiasm of youthful days. Lord Byron was conscious of this effect, and purposely cherished and brooded over the remembrance of his early passion, and of all the scenes of Annesley Hall connected with it. It was this remembrance that attuned his mind to some of its most elevated and virtuous strains, and shed an inexpressible grace and pathos over his best productions.

Being thus put upon the traces of this little love-story, I cannot refrain from threading them out, as they appear from time to time in various passages of Lord Byron's works. During his subsequent rambles in the East, when time and distance had softened away his "early romance" almost into the remembrance of a pleasing and tender dream, he received accounts of the object of it, which represented her, still in her paternal Hall, among her native bowers of Annesley, surrounded by a blooming and beautiful family, yet a prey to secret and withering melancholy--

    ----"In her home,
A thousand leagues from his,--her native home,
She dwelt, begirt with growing infancy,
Daughters and sons of beauty, but--behold!
Upon her face there was the tint of grief,
The settled shadow of an inward strife,
And an unquiet drooping of the eye,
As if its lids were charged with unshed tears."

For an instant the buried tenderness of early youth and the fluttering hopes which accompanied it, seemed to have revived in his bosom, and the idea to have flashed upon his mind that his image might be connected with her secret woes--but he rejected the thought almost as soon as formed.

    "What could her grief be?--she had all she loved,
And he who had so loved her was not there
To trouble with bad hopes, or evil wish,
Or ill repress'd affection, her pure thoughts.
What could her grief be?--she had loved him not,
Nor given him cause to deem himself beloved,
Nor could he be a part of that which prey'd
Upon her mind--a spectre of the past."

The cause of her grief was a matter of rural comment in the neighborhood of Newstead and Annesley. It was disconnected from all idea of Lord Byron, but attributed to the harsh and capricious conduct of one to whose kindness and affection she had a sacred claim. The domestic sorrows which had long preyed in secret on her heart, at length affected her intellect, and the "bright morning star of

Annesley" was eclipsed for ever.

"The lady of his love,--oh! she was changed
As by the sickness of the soul; her mind
Had wandered from its dwelling, and her eyes,
They had not their own lustre, but the look
Which is not of the earth; she was become
The queen of a fantastic realm: but her thoughts
Were combinations of disjointed things;
And forms impalpable and unperceived
Of others' sight, familiar were to hers.
And this the world calls frenzy."

Notwithstanding lapse of time, change of place, and a succession of
splendid and spirit-stirring scenes in various countries, the quiet and
gentle scene of his boyish love seems to have held a magic sway over
the recollections of Lord Byron, and the image of Mary Chaworth to have
unexpectedly obtruded itself upon his mind like some supernatural
visitation. Such was the fact on the occasion of his marriage with Miss
Milbanke; Annesley Hall and all its fond associations floated like a
vision before his thoughts, even when at the altar, and on the point of
pronouncing the nuptial vows. The circumstance is related by him with a
force and feeling that persuade us of its truth.

"A change came o'er the spirit of my dream.
The wanderer was returned.--I saw him stand
Before an altar--with a gentle bride;
Her face was fair, but was not that which made
The star-light of his boyhood;--as he stood
Even at the altar, o'er his brow there came
The self-same aspect, and the quivering shock
That in the antique oratory shook
His bosom in its solitude; and then--

As in that hour--a moment o'er his face
The tablet of unutterable thoughts
Was traced,--and then it faded as it came,
And he stood calm and quiet, and he spoke
The fitting vows, but heard not his own words,
And all things reel'd around him: he could see
Not that which was, nor that which should have been--
But the old mansion, and the accustomed hall,
And the remember'd chambers, and the place,
The day, the hour, the sunshine, and the shade,
All things pertaining to that place and hour,
And her who was his destiny, came back,
And thrust themselves between him and the light:
What business had they there at such a time?"

The history of Lord Byron's union is too well known to need narration.
The errors, and humiliations, and heart-burnings that followed upon it,
gave additional effect to the remembrance of his early passion, and
tormented him with the idea, that had he been successful in his suit to
the lovely heiress of Annesley, they might both have shared a happier
destiny. In one of his manuscripts, written long after his marriage,
having accidentally mentioned Miss Chaworth as "my M. A. C." "Alas!"
exclaims he, with a sudden burst of feeling, "why do I say *my*?
Our union would have healed feuds in which blood had been shed by our
fathers; it would have joined lands broad and rich; it would have
joined at least *one* heart, and two persons not ill-matched in
years-and--and--and--what has been the result?"

But enough of Annesley Hall and the poetical themes connected with it.
I felt as if I could linger for hours about its ruined oratory, and
silent hall, and neglected garden, and spin reveries and dream dreams,
until all became an ideal world around me. The day, however, was fast
declining, and the shadows of evening throwing deeper shades of

melancholy about the place. Taking our leave of the worthy old housekeeper, therefore, with a small compensation and many thanks for her civilities, we mounted our horses and pursued our way back to Newstead Abbey.

THE LAKE.

"Before the mansion lay a lucid lake,
    Broad as transparent, deep, and freshly fed
By a river, which its softened way did take
    in currents through the calmer water spread
Around: the wild fowl nestled in the brake
    And sedges, brooding in their liquid bed:
The woods sloped downward to its brink, and stood
    With their green faces fixed upon the flood."

Such is Lord Byron's description of one of a series of beautiful sheets of water, formed in old times by the monks by damming up the course of a small river. Here he used daily to enjoy his favorite recreations in swimming and sailing. The "wicked old Lord," in his scheme of rural devastation, had cut down all the woods that once fringed the lake; Lord Byron, on coming of age, endeavored to restore them, and a beautiful young wood, planted by him, now sweeps up from the water's edge, and clothes the hillside opposite to the Abbey. To this woody nook Colonel Wildman has given the appropriate title of "the Poet's Corner."

The lake has inherited its share of the traditions and fables connected with everything in and about the Abbey. It was a petty Mediterranean sea on which the "wicked old Lord" used to gratify his nautical tastes and humors. He had his mimic castles and fortresses along its shores, and his mimic fleets upon its waters, and used to get up mimic sea-fights. The remains of his petty fortifications still awaken the curious inquiries of visitors. In one of his vagaries, he caused a large vessel to be brought on wheels from the sea-coast and launched in the lake. The country people were surprised to see a ship thus sailing over dry land. They called to mind a saying of Mother Shipton, the famous prophet of the vulgar, that whenever a ship freighted with ling should cross Sherwood Forest, Newstead would pass out of the Byron family. The country people, who detested the old Lord, were anxious to verify the prophecy. Ling, in the dialect of Nottingham, is the name for heather; with this plant they heaped the fated bark as it passed, so that it arrived full freighted at Newstead.

The most important stories about the lake, however, relate to the treasures that are supposed to lie buried in its bosom. These may have taken their origin in a fact which actually occurred. There was one time fished up from the deep part of the lake a great eagle of molten brass, with expanded wings, standing on a pedestal or perch of the same metal. It had doubtless served as a stand or reading-desk, in the Abbey chapel, to hold a folio Bible or missal.

The sacred relic was sent to a brazier to be cleaned. As he was at work upon it, he discovered that the pedestal was hollow and composed of several pieces. Unscrewing these, he drew forth a number of parchment deeds and grants appertaining to the Abbey, and bearing the seals of Edward III. and Henry VIII., which had thus been concealed, and ultimately sunk in the lake by the friars, to substantiate their right and title to these domains at some future day.

One of the parchment scrolls thus discovered, throws rather an awkward light upon the kind of life led by the friars of Newstead. It is an indulgence granted to them for a certain number of months, in which plenary pardon is assured in advance for all kinds of crimes, among which, several of the most gross and sensual are specifically mentioned, and the weakness of the flesh to which they are prone.

After inspecting these testimonials of monkish life, in the regions of Sherwood Forest, we cease to wonder at the virtuous indignation of Robin Hood and his outlaw crew, at the sleek sensualists of the cloister:

> "I never hurt the husbandman,
> That use to till the ground,
> Nor spill their blood that range the wood
> To follow hawk and hound,
>
> "My chiefest spite to clergy is,
> Who in these days bear sway;
> With friars and monks with their fine spunks,
> I make my chiefest prey."--OLD BALLAD OF ROBIN HOOD.

The brazen eagle has been transferred to the parochial and collegiate church of Southall, about twenty miles from Newstead, where it may still be seen in the centre of the chancel, supporting, as of yore, a ponderous Bible. As to the documents it contained, they are carefully treasured up by Colonel Wildman among his other deeds and papers, in an iron chest secured by a patent lock of nine bolts, almost equal to a magic spell.

The fishing up of this brazen relic, as I have already hinted, has given rise to the tales of treasure lying at the bottom of the lake, thrown in there by the monks when they abandoned the Abbey. The favorite story is, that there is a great iron chest there filled with gold and jewels, and chalices and crucifixes. Nay, that it has been seen, when the water of the lake was unusually low. There were large iron rings at each end, but all attempts to move it were ineffectual; either the gold it contained was too ponderous, or what is more probable, it was secured by one of those magic spells usually laid upon hidden treasure. It remains, therefore, at the bottom of the lake to this day; and it is to be hoped, may one day or other be discovered by the present worthy proprietor.

ROBIN HOOD AND SHERWOOD FOREST.

While at Newstead Abbey I took great delight in riding and rambling about the neighborhood, studying out the traces of merry Sherwood Forest, and visiting the haunts of Robin Hood. The relics of the old forest are few and scattered, but as to the bold outlaw who once held a kind of freebooting sway over it, there is scarce a hill or dale, a cliff or cavern, a well or fountain, in this part of the country, that is not connected with his memory. The very names of some of the tenants on the Newstead estate, such as Beardall and Hardstaff, sound as if they may have been borne in old times by some of the stalwart fellows of the outlaw gang. One of the earliest books that captivated my fancy when a child, was a collection of Robin Hood ballads, "adorned with cuts," which I bought of an old Scotch pedler, at the cost of all my holiday money. How I devoured its pages, and gazed upon its uncouth woodcuts! For a time my mind was filled with picturings of "merry Sherwood," and the exploits and revelling of the hold foresters; and Robin Hood, Little John, Friar Tuck, and their doughty compeers, were my heroes of romance.

These early feelings were in some degree revived when I found myself in the very heart of the far-famed forest, and, as I said before, I took a kind of schoolboy delight in hunting up all traces of old Sherwood and its sylvan chivalry. One of the first of my antiquarian rambles was on horseback, in company with Colonel Wildman and his lady, who undertook to guide me to Borne of the moldering monuments of the forest. One of these stands in front of the very gate of Newstead Park, and is known throughout the country by the name of "The Pilgrim Oak." It is a venerable tree, of great size, overshadowing a wide arena of the road. Under its shade the rustics of the neighborhood have been accustomed to assemble on certain holidays, and celebrate their rural festivals. This custom had been handed down from father to son for several generations, until the oak had acquired a kind of sacred character.

The "old Lord Byron," however, in whose eyes nothing was sacred, when he laid his desolating hand on the groves and forests of Newstead, doomed likewise this traditional tree to the axe. Fortunately the good people of Nottingham heard of the danger of their favorite oak, and hastened to ransom it from destruction. They afterward made a present of it to the poet, when he came to the estate, and the Pilgrim Oak is likely to continue a rural gathering place for many coming generations.

From this magnificent and time-honored tree we continued on our sylvan research, in quest of another oak, of more ancient date and less flourishing condition. A ride of two or three miles, the latter part across open wastes, once clothed with forest, now bare and cheerless, brought us to the tree in question. It was the Oak of Ravenshead, one of the last survivors of old Sherwood, and which had evidently once held a high head in the forest; it was now a mere wreck, crazed by time, and blasted by lightning, and standing alone on a naked waste, like a ruined column in a desert.

"The scenes are desert now, and bare,
Where flourished once a forest fair,

When these waste glens with copse were lined,
And peopled with the hart and hind.
Yon lonely oak, would he could tell
The changes of his parent dell,
Since he, so gray and stubborn now,
Waved in each breeze a sapling bough.
Would he could tell how deep the shade
A thousand mingled branches made.
Here in my shade, methinks he'd say,
The mighty stag at noontide lay,
While doe, and roe, and red-deer good,
Hare bounded by through gay green-wood."

At no great distance from Ravenshead Oak is a small cave which goes by
the name of Robin Hood's stable. It is in the breast of a hill, scooped
out of brown freestone, with rude attempt at columns and arches. Within
are two niches, which served, it is said, as stalls for the bold
outlaw's horses. To this retreat he retired when hotly pursued by the
law, for the place was a secret even from his band. The cave is
overshadowed by an oak and alder, and is hardly discoverable even at
the present day; but when the country was overrun with forest it must
have been completely concealed.

There was an agreeable wildness and loneliness in a great part of our
ride. Our devious road wound down, at one time among rocky dells, by
wandering streams, and lonely pools, haunted by shy water-fowl. We
passed through a skirt of woodland, of more modern planting, but
considered a legitimate offspring of the ancient forest, and commonly
called Jock of Sherwood. In riding through these quiet, solitary
scenes, the partridge and pheasant would now and then burst upon the
wing, and the hare scud away before us.

Another of these rambling rides in quest of popular antiquities, was to a chain of rocky cliffs, called the Kirkby Crags, which skirt the Robin Hood hills. Here, leaving my horse at the foot of the crags, I scaled their rugged sides, and seated myself in a niche of the rocks, called Robin Hood's chair. It commands a wide prospect over the valley of Newstead, and here the bold outlaw is said to have taken his seat, and kept a look-out upon the roads below, watching for merchants, and bishops, and other wealthy travellers, upon whom to pounce down, like an eagle from his eyrie.

Descending from the cliffs and remounting my horse, a ride of a mile or two further along a narrow "robber path," as it was called, which wound up into the hills between perpendicular rocks, led to an artificial cavern cut in the face of a cliff, with a door and window wrought through the living stone. This bears the name of Friar Tuck's cell, or hermitage, where, according to tradition, that jovial anchorite used to make good cheer and boisterous revel with his freebooting comrades.

Such were some of the vestiges of old Sherwood and its renowned "yeomandrie," which I visited in the neighborhood of Newstead. The worthy clergyman who officiated as chaplain at the Abbey, seeing my zeal in the cause, informed me of a considerable tract of the ancient forest, still in existence about ten miles distant. There were many fine old oaks in it, he said, that had stood for centuries, but were now shattered and "stag-headed," that is to say, their upper branches were bare, and blasted, and straggling out like the antlers of, a deer. Their trunks, too, were hollow, and full of crows and jackdaws, who made them their nestling places. He occasionally rode over to the forest in the long summer evenings, and pleased himself with loitering in the twilight about the green alleys and under the venerable trees.

The description given by the chaplain made me anxious to visit this remnant of old Sherwood, and he kindly offered to be my guide and companion. We accordingly sallied forth one morning on horseback on this sylvan expedition. Our ride took us through a part of the country where King John had once held a hunting seat; the ruins of which are still to be seen. At that time the whole neighbor hood was an open royal forest, or Frank chase, as it was termed; for King John was an enemy to parks and warrens, and other inclosures, by which game was fenced in for the private benefit and recreation of the nobles and the clergy.

Here, on the brow of a gentle hill, commanding an extensive prospect of what had once been forest, stood another of those monumental trees, which, to my mind, gave a peculiar interest to this neighborhood. It was the Parliament Oak, so called in memory of an assemblage of the kind held by King John beneath its shade. The lapse of upward of six centuries had reduced this once mighty tree to a mere crumbling fragment, yet, like a gigantic torso in ancient statuary, the grandeur of the mutilated trunk gave evidence of what it had been in the days of its glory. In contemplating its mouldering remains, the fancy busied itself in calling up the scene that must have been presented beneath its shade, when this sunny hill swarmed with the pageantry of a warlike and hunting court. When silken pavilions and warrior-tents decked its crest, and royal standards, and baronial banners, and knightly pennons rolled out to the breeze. When prelates and courtiers, and steel-clad chivalry thronged round the person of the monarch, while at a distance loitered the foresters in green, and all the rural and hunting train that waited upon his sylvan sports.

> 'A thousand vassals mustered round
> With horse, and hawk, and horn, and hound;
> And through the brake the rangers stalk,
> And falc'ners hold the ready hawk;
> And foresters in green-wood trim
> Lead in the leash the greyhound grim."

Such was the phantasmagoria that presented itself for a moment to my imagination, peopling the silent place before me with empty shadows of the past. The reverie however was transient; king, courtier, and steel-clad warrior, and forester in green, with horn, and hawk, and hound, all faded again into oblivion, and I awoke to all that remained of this once stirring scene of human pomp and power--a mouldering oak, and a tradition.

"We are such stuff as dreams are made of!"

A ride of a few miles farther brought us at length among the venerable and classic shades of Sherwood, Here I was delighted to find myself in a genuine wild wood, of primitive and natural growth, so rarely to be met with in this thickly peopled and highly cultivated country. It reminded me of the aboriginal forests of my native land. I rode through natural alleys and green-wood groves, carpeted with grass and shaded by lofty and beautiful birches. What most interested me, however, was to behold around me the mighty trunks of veteran oaks, old monumental trees, the patriarchs of Sherwood Forest. They were shattered, hollow, and moss-grown, it is true, and their "leafy honors" were nearly departed; but like mouldering towers they were noble and picturesque in their decay, and gave evidence, even in their ruins, of their ancient grandeur.

As I gazed about me upon these vestiges of once "Merrie Sherwood," the picturings of my boyish fancy began to rise in my mind, and Robin Hood and his men to stand before me.

"He clothed himself in scarlet then,
  His men were all in green;
 A finer show throughout the world
  In no place could be seen.

"Good lord! it was a gallant sight
　To see them all In a row;
With every man a good broad-sword
　And eke a good yew bow."

The horn of Robin Hood again seemed to resound through the forest. I saw this sylvan chivalry, half huntsmen, half freebooters, trooping across the distant glades, or feasting and revelling beneath the trees; I was going on to embody in this way all the ballad scenes that had delighted me when a boy, when the distant sound of a wood-cutter's axe roused me from my day-dream.

The boding apprehensions which it awakened were too soon verified. I had not ridden much farther, when I came to an open space where the work of destruction was going on. Around me lay the prostrate trunks of venerable oaks, once the towering and magnificent lords of the forest, and a number of wood-cutters were hacking and hewing at another gigantic tree, just tottering to its fall.

Alas! for old Sherwood Forest: it had fallen into the possession of a noble agriculturist; a modern utilitarian, who had no feeling for poetry or forest scenery. In a little while and this glorious woodland will be laid low; its green glades be turned into sheep-walks; its legendary bowers supplanted by turnip-fields; and "Merrie Sherwood" will exist but in ballad and tradition.

"O for the poetical superstitions," thought I, "of the olden time! that shed a sanctity over every grove; that gave to each tree its tutelar genius or nymph, and threatened disaster to all who should molest the hamadryads in their leafy abodes. Alas! for the sordid propensities of modern days, when everything is coined into gold, and this once holiday planet of ours is turned into a mere 'working-day world.'"

My cobweb fancies put to flight, and my feelings out of tune, I left
the forest in a far different mood from that in which I had entered it,
and rode silently along until, on reaching the summit of a gentle
eminence, the chime of evening bells came on the breeze across the
heath from a distant village.

I paused to listen.

"They are merely the evening bells of Mansfield," said my companion.

"Of Mansfield!" Here was another of the legendary names of this storied
neighborhood, that called up early and pleasant associations. The
famous old ballad of the King and the Miller of Mansfield came at once
to mind, and the chime of the bells put me again in good humor.

A little farther on, and we were again on the traces of Robin Hood.
Here was Fountain Dale, where he had his encounter with that stalwart
shaveling Friar Tuck, who was a kind of saint militant, alternately
wearing the casque and the cowl:

> "The curtal fryar kept Fountain dale
> Seven long years and more,
> There was neither lord, knight or earl
> Could make him yield before."

The moat is still shown which is said to have surrounded the stronghold
of this jovial and fighting friar; and the place where he and Robin
Hood had their sturdy trial of strength and prowess, in the memorable
conflict which lasted

> "From ten o'clock that very day
> Until four in the afternoon,"

and ended in the treaty of fellowship. As to the hardy feats, both of sword and trencher, performed by this "curtal fryar," behold are they not recorded at length in the ancient ballads, and in the magic pages of Ivanhoe?

The evening was fast coming on, and the twilight thickening, as we rode through these haunts famous in outlaw story. A melancholy seemed to gather over the landscape as we proceeded, for our course lay by shadowy woods, and across naked heaths, and along lonely roads, marked by some of those sinister names by which the country people in England are apt to make dreary places still more dreary. The horrors of "Thieves' Wood," and the "Murderers' Stone," and "the Hag Nook," had all to be encountered in the gathering gloom of evening, and threatened to beset our path with more than mortal peril. Happily, however, we passed these ominous places unharmed, and arrived in safety at the portal of Newstead Abbey, highly satisfied with our green-wood foray.

THE ROOK CELL.

In the course of my sojourn at the Abbey, I changed my quarters from the magnificent old state apartment haunted by Sir John Byron the Little, to another in a remote corner of the ancient edifice, immediately adjoining the ruined chapel. It possessed still more interest in my eyes, from having been the sleeping apartment of Lord Byron during his residence at the Abbey. The furniture remained the same. Here was the bed in which he slept, and which he had brought with him from college; its gilded posts surmounted by coronets, giving evidence of his aristocratical feelings. Here was likewise his college sofa; and about the walls were the portraits of his favorite butler, old Joe Murray, of his fancy acquaintance, Jackson the pugilist, together with pictures of Harrow School and the College at Cambridge, at which he was educated. The bedchamber goes by the name of the Book Cell, from its vicinity to the Rookery which, since time immemorial, has maintained possession of a solemn grove adjacent to the chapel. This venerable community afforded me much food for speculation during my residence in this apartment. In the morning I used to hear them gradually waking and seeming to call each other up. After a time, the whole fraternity would be in a flutter; some balancing and swinging on the tree tops, others perched on the pinnacle of the Abbey church, or wheeling and hovering about in the air, and the ruined walls would reverberate with their incessant cawings. In this way they would linger about the rookery and its vicinity for the early part of the morning, when, having apparently mustered all their forces, called over the roll, and determined upon their line of march, they one and all would sail off in a long straggling flight to maraud the distant fields. They would forage the country for miles, and remain absent all day, excepting now and then a scout would come home, as if to see that all was well. Toward night the whole host might be seen, like a dark cloud in the distance, winging their way homeward. They came, as it were, with whoop and halloo, wheeling high in the air above the Abbey, making various evolutions before they alighted, and then keeping up an incessant cawing in the tree tops, until they gradually fell asleep.

It is remarked at the Abbey, that the rooks, though they sally forth on forays throughout the week, yet keep about the venerable edifice on Sundays, as if they had inherited a reverence for the day, from their ancient confreres, the monks. Indeed, a believer in the metempsychosis might easily imagine these Gothic-looking birds to be the embodied souls of the ancient friars still hovering about their sanctified abode.

I dislike to disturb any point of popular and poetic faith, and was loath, therefore, to question the authenticity of this mysterious reverence for the Sabbath on the part of the Newstead rooks; but certainly in the course of my sojourn in the Rook Cell, I detected them in a flagrant outbreak and foray on a bright Sunday morning.

Beside the occasional clamor of the rookery, this remote apartment was often greeted with sounds of a different kind, from the neighboring ruins. The great lancet window in front of the chapel, adjoins the very wall of the chamber; and the mysterious sounds from it at night have been well described by Lord Byron:

----"Now loud, now frantic,
  The gale sweeps through its fretwork, and oft sings
  The owl his anthem, when the silent quire
  Lie with their hallelujahs quenched like fire.

"But on the noontide of the moon, and when
  The wind is winged from one point of heaven,
There moans a strange unearthly sound, which then
  Is musical-a dying accent driven
Through the huge arch, which soars and sinks again.
  Some deem it but the distant echo given
Back to the night wind by the waterfall,
And harmonized by the old choral wall.

"Others, that some original shape or form,
  Shaped by decay perchance, hath given the power
To this gray ruin, with a voice to charm.
  Sad, but serene, it sweeps o'er tree or tower;
The cause I know not, nor can solve; but such
The fact:--I've heard it,--once perhaps too much."

Never was a traveller in quest of the romantic in greater luck. I had in sooth, got lodged in another haunted apartment of the Abbey; for in this chamber Lord Byron declared he had more than once been harassed at midnight by a mysterious visitor. A black shapeless form would sit cowering upon his bed, and after gazing at him for a time with glaring eyes, would roll off and disappear. The same uncouth apparition is said to have disturbed the slumbers of a newly married couple that once passed their honeymoon in this apartment.

I would observe, that the access to the Rook Cell is by a spiral stone staircase leading up into it, as into a turret, from, the long shadowy corridor over the cloisters, one of the midnight walks of the Goblin Friar. Indeed, to the fancies engendered in his brain in this remote and lonely apartment, incorporated with the floating superstitions of the Abbey, we are no doubt indebted for the spectral scene in "Don Juan."

"Then as the night was clear, though cold, he threw
  His chamber door wide open--and went forth
Into a gallery, of sombre hue,
  Long furnish'd with old pictures of great worth,
Of knights and dames, heroic and chaste too,
  As doubtless should be people of high birth.

"No sound except the echo of his sigh
  Or step ran sadly through that antique house,
When suddenly he heard, or thought so, nigh,
  A supernatural agent--or a mouse,
Whose little nibbling rustle will embarrass
Most people, as it plays along the arras.

"It was no mouse, but lo! a monk, arrayed
  In cowl, and beads, and dusky garb, appeared,
Now in the moonlight, and now lapsed in shade;

With steps that trod as heavy, yet unheard;
His garments only a slight murmur made;
  He moved as shadowy as the sisters weird,
But slowly; and as he passed Juan by
Glared, without pausing, on him a bright eye.

"Juan was petrified; he had heard a hint
  Of such a spirit in these halls of old,
But thought, like most men, there was nothing in't
  Beyond the rumor which such spots unfold,
Coin'd from surviving superstition's mint,
  Which passes ghosts in currency like gold,
But rarely seen, like gold compared with paper.
And did he see this? or was it a vapor?

"Once, twice, thrice pass'd, repass'd--the thing of air,
  Or earth beneath, or heaven, or t'other place;
And Juan gazed upon it with a stare,
  Yet could not speak or move; but, on its base
As stauds a statue, stood: he felt his hair
  Twine like a knot of snakes around his face;
He tax'd his tongue for words, which were not granted
To ask the reverend person what he wanted.

"The third time, after a still longer pause,
  The shadow pass'd away--but where? the hall
Was long, and thus far there was no great cause
  To think its vanishing unnatural:
Doors there were many, through which, by the laws
  Of physics, bodies, whether short or tall,
Might come or go; but Juan could not state
Through which the spectre seem'd to evaporate.

"He stood, how long he knew not, but it seem'd
  An age--expectant, powerless, with his eyes
Strain'd on the spot where first the figure gleam'd:
  Then by degrees recall'd his energies,
And would have pass'd the whole off as a dream.
  But could not wake; he was, he did surmise,
Waking already, and return'd at length
Back to his chamber, shorn of half his strength."

As I have already observed, it is difficult to determine whether Lord
Byron was really subject to the superstitious fancies which have been
imputed to him, or whether he merely amused himself by giving currency
to them among his domestics and dependents. He certainly never scrupled
to express a belief in supernatural visitations, both verbally and in
his correspondence. If such were his foible, the Rook Cell was an
admirable place to engender these delusions. As I have lain awake at
night, I have heard all kinds of mysterious and sighing sounds from the
neighboring ruin. Distant footsteps, too, and the closing of doors in
remote parts of the Abbey, would send hollow reverberations and echoes
along the corridor and up the spiral staircase. Once, in fact, I was
roused by a strange sound at the very door of my chamber. I threw it
open, and a form "black and shapeless with glaring eyes" stood before
me. It proved, however, neither ghost nor goblin, but my friend
Boatswain, the great Newfoundland dog, who had conceived a
companionable liking for me, and occasionally sought me in my
apartment. To the hauntings of even such a visitant as honest Boatswain
may we attribute some of the marvellous stories about the Goblin Friar.

THE LITTLE WHITE LADY.

In the course of a morning's ride with Colonel Wildman, about the Abbey lands, we found ourselves in one of the prettiest little wild woods imaginable. The road to it had led us among rocky ravines overhung with thickets, and now wound through birchen dingles and among beautiful groves and clumps of elms and beeches. A limpid rill of sparkling water, winding and doubling in perplexed mazes, crossed our path repeatedly, so as to give the wood the appearance of being watered by numerous rivulets. The solitary and romantic look of this piece of woodland, and the frequent recurrence of its mazy stream, put him in mind, Colonel Wildman said, of the little German fairy tale of Undine, in which is recorded the adventures of a knight who had married a water-nymph. As he rode with his bride through her native woods, every stream claimed her as a relative; one was a brother, another an uncle, another a cousin. We rode on amusing ourselves with applying this fanciful tale to the charming scenery around us, until we came to a lowly gray-stone farmhouse, of ancient date, situated in a solitary glen, on the margin of the brook, and overshadowed by venerable trees. It went by the name, as I was told, of the Weir Mill farmhouse. With this rustic mansion was connected a little tale of real life, some circumstances of which were related to me on the spot, and others I collected in the course of my sojourn at the Abbey.

Not long after Colonel Wildman had purchased the estate of Newstead, he made it a visit for the purpose of planning repairs and alterations. As he was rambling one evening, about dusk, in company with his architect, through this little piece of woodland, he was struck with its peculiar characteristics, and then, for the first time, compared it to the haunted wood of Undine. While he was making the remark, a small female figure in white, flitted by without speaking a word, or indeed appearing to notice them. Her step was scarcely heard as she passed, and her form was indistinct in the twilight.

"What a figure for a fairy or sprite!" exclaimed Colonel Wildman. "How much a poet or a romance writer would make of such an apparition, at such a time and in such a place!"

He began to congratulate himself upon having some elfin inhabitant for his haunted wood, when, on proceeding a few paces, he found a white frill lying in the path, which had evidently fallen from the figure that had just passed.

"Well," said he, "after all, this is neither sprite nor fairy, but a being of flesh, and blood, and muslin."

Continuing on, he came to where the road passed by an old mill in front of the Abbey. The people of the mill were at the door. He paused and inquired whether any visitor had been at the Abbey, but was answered in the negative.

"Has nobody passed by here?"

"No one, sir."

"That's strange! Surely I met a female in white, who must have passed along this path."

"Oh, sir, you mean the Little White Lady--oh, yes, she passed by here not long since."

"The Little White Lady! And pray who is the Little White Lady?"

"Why, sir, that nobody knows; she lives in the Weir Mill farmhouse, down in the skirts of the wood. She comes to the Abbey every morning, keeps about it all day, and goes away at night. She speaks to nobody, and we are rather shy of her, for we don't know what to make of her."

Colonel Wildman now concluded that it was some artist or amateur employed in making sketches of the Abbey, and thought no more about the matter. He went to London, and was absent for some time. In the interim, his sister, who was newly married, came with her husband to pass the honeymoon at the Abbey. The Little White Lady still resided in the Weir Mill farmhouse, on the border of the haunted wood, and continued her visits daily to the Abbey. Her dress was always the same, a white gown with a little black spencer or bodice, and a white hat with a short veil that screened the upper part of her countenance. Her habits were shy, lonely, and silent; she spoke to no one, and sought no companionship, excepting with the Newfoundland dog that had belonged to Lord Byron. His friendship she secured by caressing him and occasionally bringing him food, and he became the companion of her solitary walks. She avoided all strangers, and wandered about the retired parts of the garden; sometimes sitting for hours by the tree on which Lord Byron had carved his name, or at the foot of the monument which he had erected among the ruins of the chapel. Sometimes she read, sometimes she wrote with a pencil on a small slate which she carried with her, but much of her time was passed in a kind of reverie.

The people about the place gradually became accustomed to her, and suffered her to wander about unmolested; their distrust of her subsided on discovering that most of her peculiar and lonely habits arose from the misfortune of being deaf and dumb. Still she was regarded with some degree of shyness, for it was the common opinion that she was not exactly in her right mind.

Colonel Wildman's sister was informed of all these circumstances by the servants of the Abbey, among whom the Little White Lady was a theme of frequent discussion. The Abbey and its monastic environs being haunted ground, it was natural that a mysterious visitant of the kind, and one supposed to be under the influence of mental hallucination, should inspire awe in a person unaccustomed to the place. As Colonel Wildman's sister was one day walking along abroad terrace of the garden, she suddenly beheld the Little White Lady coming toward her, and, in the surprise and agitation of the moment, turned and ran into the house. Day after day now elapsed, and nothing more was seen of this singular personage. Colonel Wildman at length arrived at the Abbey, and his sister mentioned to him her encounter and fright in the garden. It brought to mind his own adventure with the Little White Lady in the wood of Undine, and he was surprised to find that she still continued her mysterious wanderings about the Abbey. The mystery was soon explained. Immediately after his arrival he received a letter written in the most minute and delicate female hand, and in elegant and even eloquent language. It was from the Little White Lady. She had noticed and been shocked by the abrupt retreat of Colonel Wildman's sister on seeing her in the garden walk, and expressed her unhappiness at being an object of alarm to any of his family. She explained the motives of her frequent and long visits to the Abbey, which proved to be a singularly enthusiastic idolatry of the genius of Lord Byron, and a solitary and passionate delight in haunting the scenes he had once inhabited. She hinted at the infirmities which cut her off from all social communion with her fellow beings, and at her situation in life as desolate and bereaved; and concluded by hoping that he would not deprive her of her only comfort, the permission of visiting the Abbey occasionally, and lingering about the walks and gardens.

Colonel Wildman now made further inquiries concerning her, and found that she was a great favorite with the people of the farmhouse where she boarded, from the gentleness, quietude, and innocence of her manners. When at home, she passed the greater part of her time in a small sitting-room, reading and writing. Colonel Wildman immediately

called on her at the farmhouse. She received him with some agitation
and embarrassment, but his frankness and urbanity soon put her at her
ease. She was past the bloom of youth, a pale, nervous little being,
and apparently deficient in most of her physical organs, for in
addition to being deaf and dumb, she saw but imperfectly. They carried
on a communication by means of a small slate, which she drew out of her
reticule, and on which they wrote their questions and replies. In
writing or reading she always approached her eyes close to the written
characters.

This defective organization was accompanied by a morbid sensibility
almost amounting to disease. She had not been born deaf and dumb; but
had lost her hearing in a fit of sickness, and with it the power of
distinct articulation. Her life had evidently been checkered and
unhappy; she was apparently without family or friend, a lonely,
desolate being, cut off from society by her infirmities.

"I am always among strangers," she said, "as much so in my native
country as I could be in the remotest parts of the world. By all I am
considered as a stranger and an alien; no one will acknowledge any
connection with me. I seem not to belong to the human species."

Such were the circumstances that Colonel Wildman was able to draw forth
in the course of his conversation, and they strongly interested him in
favor of this poor enthusiast. He was too devout an admirer of Lord
Byron himself, not to sympathize in this extraordinary zeal of one of
his votaries, and he entreated her to renew her visits at the Abbey,
assuring her that the edifice and its grounds should always be open to
her.

The Little White Lady now resumed her daily walks in the Monk's Garden,
and her occasional seat at the foot of the monument; she was shy and
diffident, however, and evidently fearful of intruding. If any persons

were walking in the garden she would avoid them, and seek the most remote parts; and was seen like a sprite, only by gleams and glimpses, as she glided among the groves and thickets. Many of her feelings and fancies, during these lonely rambles, were embodied in verse, noted down on her tablet, and transferred to paper in the evening on her return to the farmhouse. Some of these verses now lie before me, written with considerable harmony of versification, but chiefly curious as being illustrative of that singular and enthusiastic idolatry with which she almost worshipped the genius of Byron, or rather, the romantic image of him formed by her imagination.

Two or three extracts may not be unacceptable. The following are from a long rhapsody addressed to Lord Byron:

"By what dread charm thou rulest the mind
  It is not given for us to know;
We glow with feelings undefined,
  Nor can explain from whence they flow.

"Not that fond love which passion breathes
  And youthful hearts inflame;
The soul a nobler homage gives,
  And bows to thy great name.

"Oft have we own'd the muses' skill,
  And proved the power of song,
But sweeter notes ne'er woke the thrill
  That solely to thy verse belong.

"This--but far more, for thee we prove,
  Something that bears a holier name,
Than the pure dream of early love,
  Or friendship's nobler flame.

"Something divine--Oh! what it is
  Thy muse alone can tell,
So sweet, but so profound the bliss
  We dread to break the spell."

This singular and romantic infatuation, for such it might truly be called, was entirely spiritual and ideal, for, as she herself declares in another of her rhapsodies, she had never beheld Lord Byron; he was, to her, a mere phantom of the brain.

"I ne'er have drunk thy glance--thy form
  My earthly eye has never seen,
Though oft when fancy's visions warm,
  It greets me in some blissful dream.

"Greets me, as greets the sainted seer
  Some radiant visitant from high,
When heaven's own strains break on his ear,
  And wrap his soul in ecstasy."

Her poetical wanderings and musings were not confined to the Abbey grounds, but extended to all parts of the neighborhood connected with the memory of Lord Byron, and among the rest to the groves and gardens of Annesley Hall, the seat of his early passion for Miss Chaworth. One of her poetical effusions mentions her having seen from Howet's Hill in Annesley Park, a "sylph-like form," in a car drawn by milk-white horses, passing by the foot of the hill, who proved to be the "favorite child," seen by Lord Byron, in his memorable interview with Miss Chaworth after her marriage. That favorite child was now a blooming girl approaching to womanhood, and seems to have understood something of the character and story of this singular visitant, and to have treated her with gentle sympathy. The Little White Lady expresses, in touching terms, in a note to her verses, her sense of this gentle courtesy. "The benevolent condescension," says she, "of that amiable and interesting young lady, to the unfortunate writer of these simple lines will remain engraved upon a grateful memory, till the vital spark that now animates a heart that too sensibly feels, and too seldom experiences such kindness, is forever extinct."

In the mean time, Colonel Wildman, in occasional interviews, had obtained further particulars of the story of the stranger, and found that poverty was added to the other evils of her forlorn and isolated state. Her name was Sophia Hyatt. She was the daughter of a country bookseller, but both her parents had died several years before. At their death, her sole dependence was upon her brother, who allowed her a small annuity on her share of the property left by their father, and which remained in his hands. Her brother, who was a captain of a merchant vessel, removed with his family to America, leaving her almost alone in the world, for she had no other relative in England but a cousin, of whom she knew almost nothing. She received her annuity regularly for a time, but unfortunately her brother died in the West Indies, leaving his affairs in confusion, and his estate overhung by several commercial claims, which threatened to swallow up the whole. Under these disastrous circumstances, her annuity suddenly ceased; she had in vain tried to obtain a renewal of it from the widow, or even an account of the state of her brother's affairs. Her letters for three years past had remained unanswered, and she would have been exposed to the horrors of the most abject want, but for a pittance quarterly doled out to her by her cousin in England.

Colonel Wildman entered with characteristic benevolence into the story of her troubles. He saw that she was a helpless, unprotected being, unable, from her infirmities and her ignorance of the world, to prosecute her just claims. He obtained from her the address of her relations in America, and of the commercial connection of her brother;

promised, through the medium of his own agents in Liverpool, to institute an inquiry into the situation of her brother's affairs, and to forward any letters she might write, so as to insure their reaching their place of destination.

Inspired with some faint hopes, the Little White Lady continued her wanderings about the Abbey and its neighborhood. The delicacy and timidity of her deportment increased the interest already felt for her by Mrs. Wildman. That lady, with her wonted kindness, sought to make acquaintance with her, and inspire her with confidence. She invited her into the Abbey; treated her with the most delicate attention, and, seeing that she had a great turn for reading, offered her the loan of any books in her possession. She borrowed a few, particularly the works of Sir Walter Scott, but soon returned them; the writings of Lord Byron seemed to form the only study in which she delighted, and when not occupied in reading those, her time was passed in passionate meditations on his genius. Her enthusiasm spread an ideal world around her in which she moved and existed as in a dream, forgetful at times of the real miseries which beset her in her mortal state.

One of her rhapsodies is, however, of a very melancholy cast; anticipating her own death, which her fragile frame and growing infirmities rendered but too probable. It is headed by the following paragraph.

"Written beneath the tree on Crowholt Hill, where it is my wish to be interred (if I should die in Newstead)."

I subjoin a few of the stanzas: they are addressed to Lord Byron:

"Thou, while thou stand'st beneath this tree,
  While by thy foot this earth is press'd,
Think, here the wanderer's ashes be--

And wilt thou say, sweet be thy rest!

"'Twould add even to a seraph's bliss,
  Whose sacred charge thou then may be,
To guide--to guard--yes, Byron! yes,
  That glory is reserved for me."

"If woes below may plead above
  A frail heart's errors, mine forgiven,
To that 'high world' I soar, where 'love
  Surviving' forms the bliss of Heaven.

"O wheresoe'er, in realms above,
  Assign'd my spirit's new abode,
'Twill watch thee with a seraph's love,
  Till thou too soar'st to meet thy God.

"And here, beneath this lonely tree--
  Beneath the earth thy feet have press'd,
My dust shall sleep--once dear to thee
  These scenes--here may the wanderer rest!"

In the midst of her reveries and rhapsodies, tidings reached Newstead
of the untimely death of Lord Byron. How they were received by this
humble but passionate devotee I could not ascertain; her life was too
obscure and lonely to furnish much personal anecdote, but among her
poetical effusions are several written in a broken and irregular
manner, and evidently under great agitation.

The following sonnet is the most coherent and most descriptive of her
peculiar state of mind:

  "Well, thou art gone--but what wert thou to me?

I never saw thee--never heard thy voice,
Yet my soul seemed to claim affiance with thee.
   The Roman bard has sung of fields Elysian,
Where the soul sojourns ere she visits earth;
   Sure it was there my spirit knew thee, Byron!
Thine image haunted me like a past vision;
   It hath enshrined itself in my heart's core;
'Tis my soul's soul--it fills the whole creation.
   For I do live but in that world ideal
Which the muse peopled with her bright fancies,
   And of that world thou art a monarch real,
Nor ever earthly sceptre ruled a kingdom,
   With sway so potent as thy lyre, the mind's dominion."

Taking all the circumstances here adduced into consideration, it is
evident that this strong excitement and exclusive occupation of the
mind upon one subject, operating upon a system in a high state of
morbid irritability, was in danger of producing that species of mental
derangement called monomania. The poor little being was aware, herself,
of the dangers of her case, and alluded to it in the following passage
of a letter to Colonel Wildman, which presents one of the most
lamentable pictures of anticipated evil ever conjured up by the human
mind.

"I have long," writes she, "too sensibly felt the decay of my mental
faculties, which I consider as the certain indication of that dreaded
calamity which I anticipate with such terror. A strange idea has long
haunted my mind, that Swift's dreadful fate will be mine. It is not
ordinary insanity I so much apprehend, but something worse--absolute
idiotism!

"O sir! think what I must suffer from such an idea, without an earthly
friend to look up to for protection in such a wretched state--exposed

to the indecent insults which such spectacles always excite. But I dare not dwell upon the thought: it would facilitate the event I so much dread, and contemplate with horror. Yet I cannot help thinking from people's behavior to me at times, and from after reflections upon my conduct, that symptoms of the disease are already apparent."

Five months passed away, but the letters written by her, and forwarded by Colonel Wildman to America relative to her brother's affairs, remained unanswered; the inquiries instituted by the Colonel had as yet proved equally fruitless. A deeper gloom and despondency now seemed to gather upon her mind. She began to talk of leaving Newstead, and repairing to London, in the vague hope of obtaining relief or redress by instituting some legal process to ascertain and enforce the will of her deceased brother. Weeks elapsed, however, before she could summon up sufficient resolution to tear herself away from the scene of poetical fascination. The following simple stanzas, selected from a number written about the time, express, in humble rhymes, the melancholy that preyed upon her spirits:

"Farewell to thee, Newstead, thy time-riven towers,
　Shall meet the fond gaze of the pilgrim no more;
No more may she roam through thy walks and thy bowers.
　Nor muse in thy cloisters at eve's pensive hour.

"Oh, how shall I leave you, ye hills and ye dales,
　When lost in sad musing, though sad not unblest,
A lone pilgrim I stray--Ah! in these lonely vales,
　I hoped, vainly hoped, that the pilgrim might rest.

"Yet rest is far distant--in the dark vale of death,
　Alone I shall find it, an outcast forlorn--
But hence vain complaints, though by fortune bereft
　Of all that could solace in life's early morn.

Is not man from his birth doomed a pilgrim to roam
  O'er the world's dreary wilds, whence by fortune's rude gust.
In his path, if some flowret of joy chanced to bloom,
  It is torn and its foliage laid low in the dust."

At length she fixed upon a day for her departure. On the day previous, she paid a farewell visit to the Abbey; wandering over every part of the grounds and garden; pausing and lingering at every place particularly associated with the recollection of Lord Byron; and passing a long time seated at the foot of the monument, which she used to call "her altar." Seeking Mrs. Wildman, she placed in her hands a sealed packet, with an earnest request that she would not open it until after her departure from the neighborhood. This done she took an affectionate leave of her, and with many bitter tears bade farewell to the Abbey.

On retiring to her room that evening, Mrs. Wildman could not refrain from inspecting the legacy of this singular being. On opening the packet, she found a number of fugitive poems, written in a most delicate and minute hand, and evidently the fruits of her reveries and meditations during her lonely rambles; from these the foregoing extracts have been made. These were accompanied by a voluminous letter, written with the pathos and eloquence of genuine feeling, and depicting her peculiar situation and singular state of mind in dark but painful colors.

"The last time," says she, "that I had the pleasure of seeing you, in the garden, you asked me why I leave Newstead; when I told you my circumstances obliged me, the expression of concern which I fancied I observed in your look and manner would have encouraged me to have been explicit at the time, but from my inability of expressing myself verbally."

She then goes on to detail precisely her pecuniary circumstances, by which it appears that her whole dependence for subsistence was on an allowance of thirteen pounds a year from her cousin, who bestowed it through a feeling of pride, lest his relative should come upon the parish. During two years this pittance had been augmented from other sources, to twenty-three pounds, but the last year it had shrunk within its original bounds, and was yielded so grudgingly, that she could not feel sure of its continuance from one quarter to another. More than once it had been withheld on slight pretences, and she was in constant dread lest it should be entirely withdrawn.

"It is with extreme reluctance," observed she, "that I have so far exposed my unfortunate situation; but I thought you expected to know something more of it, and I feared that Colonel Wildman, deceived by appearances, might think that I am in no immediate want, and that the delay of a few weeks, or months, respecting the inquiry, can be of no material consequence. It is absolutely necessary to the success of the business that Colonel Wildman should know the exact state of my circumstances without reserve, that he may be enabled to make a correct representation of them to any gentleman whom he intends to interest, who, I presume, if they are not of America themselves, have some connections there, through whom my friends may be convinced of the reality of my distress, if they pretend to doubt it, as I suppose they do. But to be more explicit is impossible; it would be too humiliating to particularize the circumstances of the embarrassment in which I am unhappily involved--my utter destitution. To disclose all might, too, be liable to an inference which I hope I am not so void of delicacy, of natural pride, as to endure the thought of. Pardon me, madam, for thus giving trouble, where I have no right to do--compelled to throw myself upon Colonel Wildman's humanity, to entreat his earnest exertions in my behalf, for it is now my only resource. Yet do not too much despise me for thus submitting to imperious necessity--it is not love of life, believe me it is not, nor anxiety for its preservation. I cannot say, 'There are things that make the world dear to me,'--for in the world there is not an object to make me wish to linger here another hour, could I find that rest and peace in the grave which I have never found on earth, and I fear will be denied me there."

Another part of her letter develops more completely the dark despondency hinted at in the conclusion of the foregoing extract--and presents a lamentable instance of a mind diseased, which sought in vain, amidst sorrow and calamity, the sweet consolations of religious faith.

"That my existence has hitherto been prolonged," says she, "often beyond what I have thought to have been its destined period, is astonishing to myself. Often when my situation has been as desperate, as hopeless, or more so, if possible, than it is at present, some unexpected interposition of Providence has rescued me from a fate that has appeared inevitable. I do not particularly allude to recent circumstances or latter years, for from my earlier years I have been the child of Providence--then why should I distrust its care now? I do not *dis*trust it--neither do I trust it. I feel perfectly unanxious, unconcerned, and indifferent as to the future; but this is not trust in Providence--not that trust which alone claims it protections. I know this is a blamable indifference--it is more--for it reaches to the interminable future. It turns almost with disgust from the bright prospects which religion offers for the consolation and support of the wretched, and to which I was early taught, by an almost adored mother, to look forward with hope and joy; but to me they can afford no consolation. Not that I doubt the sacred truths that religion inculcates. I cannot doubt--though I confess I have sometimes tried to do so, because I no longer wish for that immortality of which it assures us. My only wish now is for rest and peace--endless rest. 'For rest--but not to feel 'tis rest,' but I cannot delude myself with the hope that such rest will be my lot. I feel an internal evidence, stronger than any arguments that reason or religion can enforce, that I have that within me which is imperishable; that drew not its origin from the 'clod of the valley.' With this conviction, but without a hope to brighten the prospect of that dread future:

"'I dare not look beyond the tomb, Yet cannot hope for peace before.' Such an unhappy frame of mind, I am sure, madam, must excite your commiseration. It is perhaps owing, in part at least, to the solitude in which I have lived, I may say, even in the midst of society; when I have mixed in it; as my infirmities entirely exclude me from that sweet intercourse of kindred spirits--that sweet solace of refined conversation; the little intercourse I have at any time with those around me cannot be termed conversation--they are not kindred spirits-- and even where circumstances have associated me (but rarely indeed) with superior and cultivated minds, who have not disdained to admit me to their society, they could not by all their generous efforts, even in early youth, lure from my dark soul the thoughts that loved to lie buried there, nor inspire me with the courage to attempt their disclosure; and yet of all the pleasures of polished life which fancy has often pictured to me in such vivid colors, there is not one that I have so ardently coveted as that sweep reciprocation of ideas, the supreme bliss of enlightened minds in the hour of social converse. But this I knew was not decreed for me--

  "'Yet this was in my nature-'

but since the loss of my hearing I have always been incapable of verbal conversation. I need not, however, inform you, madam, of this. At the first interview with which you favored me, you quickly discovered my peculiar unhappiness in this respect; you perceived from my manner that any attempt to draw me into conversation would be in vain--had it been otherwise, perhaps you would not have disdained now and then to have soothed the lonely wanderer with yours. I have sometimes fancied when I have seen you in the walk, that you seemed to wish to encourage me to throw myself in your way. Pardon me if my imagination, too apt to beguile me with such dear illusions, has deceived me into too presumptuous an idea here. You must have observed that I generally endeavored to avoid both you and Colonel Wildman. It was to spare your generous hearts the pain of witnessing distress you could not alleviate. Thus cut off, as it were, from all human society, I have been compelled to live in a world of my own, and certainly with the beings with which my world is peopled, I am at no loss to converse. But, though I love solitude and am never in want of subjects to amuse my fancy, yet solitude too much indulged in must necessarily have an unhappy effect upon the mind, which, when left to seek for resources wholly within itself will, unavoidably, in hours of gloom and despondency, brood over corroding thoughts that prey upon the spirits, and sometimes terminate in confirmed misanthropy--especially with those who, from constitution, or early misfortunes, are inclined to melancholy, and to view human nature in its dark shades. And have I not cause for gloomy reflections? The utter loneliness of my lot would alone have rendered existence a curse to one whom nature has formed glowing with all the warmth of social affection, yet without an object on which to place it--without one natural connection, one earthly friend to appeal to, to shield me from the contempt, indignities, and insults, to which my deserted situation continually exposed me."

I am giving long extracts from this letter, yet I cannot refrain from subjoining another letter, which depicts her feelings with respect to Newstead.

"Permit me, madame, again to request your and Colonel Wildman's acceptance of these acknowledgments which I cannot too often repeat, for your unexampled goodness to a rude stranger. I know I ought not to have taken advantage of your extreme good nature so frequently as I

have. I should have absented myself from your garden during the stay of
the company at the Abbey, but, as I knew I must be gone long before
they would leave it, I could not deny myself the indulgence, as you so
freely gave me your permission to continue my walks, but now they are
at an end. I have taken my last farewell of every dear and interesting
spot, which I now never hope to see again, unless my disembodied spirit
may be permitted to revisit them.--Yet O! if Providence should enable
me again to support myself with any degree of respectability, and you
should grant me some little humble shed, with what joy shall I return
and renew my delightful rambles. But dear as Newstead is to me, I will
never again come under the same unhappy circumstances as I have this
last time--never without the means of at least securing myself from
contempt. How dear, how very dear Newstead is to me, how unconquerable
the infatuation that possesses me, I am now going to give a too
convincing proof. In offering to your acceptance the worthless trifles
that will accompany this, I hope you will believe that I have no view
to your amusement. I dare not hope that the consideration of their
being the products of your own garden, and most of them written there,
in my little tablet, while sitting at the foot of ***my Altar***--I
could not, I cannot resist the earnest desire of leaving this memorial
of the many happy hours I have there enjoyed. Oh! do not reject them,
madam; suffer them to remain with you, and if you should deign to honor
them with a perusal, when you read them repress, if you can, the smile
that I know will too naturally arise, when you recollect the appearance
of the wretched being who has dared to devote her whole soul to the
contemplation of such more than human excellence. Yet, ridiculous as
such devotion may appear to some, I must take leave to say, that if the
sentiments which I have entertained for that exalted being could be
duly appreciated, I trust they would be found to be of such a nature as
is no dishonor even for him to have inspired."...

"I am now coming to take a last, last view of scenes too deeply
impressed upon my memory ever to be effaced even by madness itself. O

madam! may you never know, nor be able to conceive the agony I endure
in tearing myself from all that the world contains of dear and sacred
to me: the only spot on earth where I can ever hope for peace or
comfort. May every blessing the world has to bestow attend you, or
rather, may you long, long live in the enjoyment of the delights of
your own paradise, in secret seclusion from a world that has no real
blessings to bestow. Now I go--but O might I dare to hope that when you
are enjoying these blissful scenes, a thought of the unhappy wanderer
might sometimes cross your mind, how soothing would such an idea be, if
I dared to indulge it--could you see my heart at this moment, how
needless would it be to assure you of the respectful gratitude, the
affectionate esteem, this heart must ever bear you both."

The effect of this letter upon the sensitive heart of Mrs. Wildman may
be more readily conceived than expressed. Her first impulse was to give
a home to this poor homeless being, and to fix her in the midst of
those scenes which formed her earthly paradise. She communicated her
wishes to Colonel Wildman, and they met with an immediate response in
his generous bosom. It was settled on the spot, that an apartment
should be fitted up for the Little White Lady in one of the new
farmhouses, and every arrangement made for her comfortable and
permanent maintenance on the estate. With a woman's prompt benevolence,
Mrs. Wildman, before she laid her head upon her pillow, wrote the
following letter to the destitute stranger:

"NEWSTEAD ABBEY,
  "Tuesday night, September 20, 1825.

"On retiring to my bedchamber this evening I have opened your letter,
and cannot lose a moment in expressing to you the strong interest which
it has excited both in Colonel Wildman and myself, from the details of
your peculiar situation, and the delicate, and, let me add, elegant
language in which they are conveyed. I am anxious that my note should

reach you previous to your departure from this neighborhood, and should
be truly happy if, by any arrangement for your accommodation, I could
prevent the necessity of your undertaking the journey. Colonel Wildman
begs me to assure you that he will use his best exertions in the
investigation of those matters which you have confided to him, and
should you remain here at present, or return again after a short
absence, I trust we shall find means to become better acquainted, and
to convince you of the interest I feel, and the real satisfaction it
would afford me to contribute in any way to your comfort and happiness.
I will only now add my thanks for the little packet which I received
with your letter, and I must confess that the letter has so entirely
engaged my attention, that I have not as yet had time for the attentive
perusal of its companion.

Believe me, dear madam, with sincere good wishes,

"Yours truly,
"LOUISA WILDMAN."

Early the next morning a servant was dispatched with the letter to the
Weir Mill farm, but returned with the information that the Little White
Lady had set off, before his arrival, in company with the farmer's
wife, in a cart for Nottingham, to take her place in the coach for
London. Mrs. Wildman ordered him to mount horse instantly, follow with
all speed, and deliver the letter into her hand before the departure of
the coach.

The bearer of good tidings spared neither whip nor spur, and arrived at
Nottingham on a gallop. On entering the town, a crowd obstructed him in
the principal street. He checked his horse to make his way through it
quietly. As the crowd opened to the right and left, he beheld a human
body lying on the pavement.--It was the corpse of the Little White
Lady!

It seems that on arriving in town and dismounting from the cart, the farmer's wife had parted with her to go on an errand, and the White Lady continued on toward the coach-office. In crossing a street a cart came along, driven at a rapid rate. The driver called out to her, but she was too deaf to hear his voice or the rattling of his cart. In an instant she was knocked down by the horse, and the wheels passed over her body, and she died without a groan.

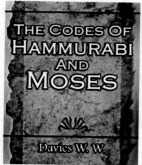

The Codes Of Hammurabi And Moses
W. W. Davies

The discovery of the Hammurabi Code is one of the greatest achievements of archaeology, and is of paramount interest, not only to the student of the Bible, but also to all those interested in ancient history...

Religion   ISBN: *1-59462-338-4*

QTY

Pages:132

MSRP $12.95

The Theory of Moral Sentiments
Adam Smith

This work from 1749. contains original theories of conscience amd moral judgment and it is the foundation for systemof morals.

Philosophy   ISBN: *1-59462-777-0*

QTY

Pages:536

MSRP $19.95

Jessica's First Prayer
Hesba Stretton

In a screened and secluded corner of one of the many railway-bridges which span the streets of London there could be seen a few years ago, from five o'clock every morning until half past eight, a tidily set-out coffee-stall, consisting of a trestle and board, upon which stood two large tin cans, with a small fire of charcoal burning under each so as to keep the coffee boiling during the early hours of the morning when the work-people were thronging into the city on their way to their daily toil...

QTY

Pages:84

Childrens   ISBN: *1-59462-373-2*

MSRP $9.95

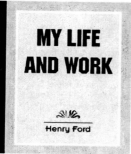

My Life and Work
Henry Ford

Henry Ford revolutionized the world with his implementation of mass production for the Model T automobile. Gain valuable business insight into his life and work with his own auto-biography... "We have only started on our development of our country we have not as yet, with all our talk of wonderful progress, done more than scratch the surface. The progress has been wonderful enough but..."

QTY

Pages:300

Biographies/   ISBN: *1-59462-198-5*

MSRP $21.95

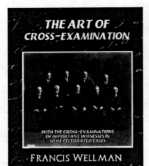

The Art of Cross-Examination
Francis Wellman

QTY

I presume it is the experience of every author, after his first book is published upon an important subject, to be almost overwhelmed with a wealth of ideas and illustrations which could readily have been included in his book, and which to his own mind, at least, seem to make a second edition inevitable. Such certainly was the case with me; and when the first edition had reached its sixth impression in five months, I rejoiced to learn that it seemed to my publishers that the book had met with a sufficiently favorable reception to justify a second and considerably enlarged edition. ..

Pages:412

Reference   ISBN: *1-59462-647-2*   *MSRP $19.95*

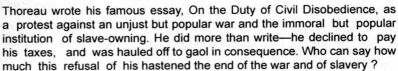

On the Duty of Civil Disobedience
Henry David Thoreau

QTY

Thoreau wrote his famous essay, On the Duty of Civil Disobedience, as a protest against an unjust but popular war and the immoral but popular institution of slave-owning. He did more than write—he declined to pay his taxes, and was hauled off to gaol in consequence. Who can say how much this refusal of his hastened the end of the war and of slavery ?

Law   ISBN: *1-59462-747-9*   **Pages:48**

MSRP $7.45

Dream Psychology Psychoanalysis for Beginners
Sigmund Freud

QTY

Sigmund Freud, born Sigismund Schlomo Freud (May 6, 1856 - September 23, 1939), was a Jewish-Austrian neurologist and psychiatrist who co-founded the psychoanalytic school of psychology. Freud is best known for his theories of the unconscious mind, especially involving the mechanism of repression; his redefinition of sexual desire as mobile and directed towards a wide variety of objects; and his therapeutic techniques, especially his understanding of transference in the therapeutic relationship and the presumed value of dreams as sources of insight into unconscious desires.

Pages:196

Psychology   ISBN: *1-59462-905-6*   *MSRP $15.45*

The Miracle of Right Thought
Orison Swett Marden

QTY

Believe with all of your heart that you will do what you were made to do. When the mind has once formed the habit of holding cheerful, happy, prosperous pictures, it will not be easy to form the opposite habit. It does not matter how improbable or how far away this realization may see, or how dark the prospects may be, if we visualize them as best we can, as vividly as possible, hold tenaciously to them and vigorously struggle to attain them, they will gradually become actualized, realized in the life. But a desire, a longing without endeavor, a yearning abandoned or held indifferently will vanish without realization.

Pages:360

Self Help   ISBN: *1-59462-644-8*   *MSRP $25.45*

QTY

The Rosicrucian Cosmo-Conception Mystic Christianity *by Max Heindel*   ISBN: *1-59462-188-8* **$38.95**
The Rosicrucian Cosmo-conception is not dogmatic, neither does it appeal to any other authority than the reason of the student. It is: not controversial, but is: sent forth in the, hope that it may help to clear...   New Age/Religion Pages 646

Abandonment To Divine Providence *by Jean-Pierre de Caussade*   ISBN: *1-59462-228-0* **$25.95**
"The Rev. Jean Pierre de Caussade was one of the most remarkable spiritual writers of the Society of Jesus in France in the 18th Century. His death took place at Toulouse in 1751. His works have gone through many editions and have been republished...   Inspirational/Religion Pages 400

Mental Chemistry *by Charles Haanel*   ISBN: *1-59462-192-6* **$23.95**
Mental Chemistry allows the change of material conditions by combining and appropriately utilizing the power of the mind. Much like applied chemistry creates something new and unique out of careful combinations of chemicals the mastery of mental chemistry...   New Age Pages 354

The Letters of Robert Browning and Elizabeth Barret Barrett 1845-1846 vol II   ISBN: *1-59462-193-4* **$35.95**
by Robert Browning and Elizabeth Barrett   Biographies Pages 596

Gleanings In Genesis (volume I) *by Arthur W. Pink*   ISBN: *1-59462-130-6* **$27.45**
Appropriately has Genesis been termed "the seed plot of the Bible" for in it we have, in germ form, almost all of the great doctrines which are afterwards fully developed in the books of Scripture which follow...   Religion/Inspirational Pages 420

The Master Key *by L. W. de Laurence*   ISBN: *1-59462-001-6* **$30.95**
In no branch of human knowledge has there been a more lively increase of the spirit of research during the past few years than in the study of Psychology, Concentration and Mental Discipline. The requests for authentic lessons in Thought Control, Mental Discipline and...   New Age/Business Pages 422

The Lesser Key Of Solomon Goetia *by L. W. de Laurence*   ISBN: *1-59462-092-X* **$9.95**
This translation of the first book of the "Lernegton" which is now for the first time made accessible to students of Talismanic Magic was done, after careful collation and edition, from numerous Ancient Manuscripts in Hebrew, Latin, and French...   New Age/Occult Pages 92

Rubaiyat Of Omar Khayyam *by Edward Fitzgerald*   ISBN: *1-59462-332-5* **$13.95**
Edward Fitzgerald, whom the world has already learned, in spite of his own efforts to remain within the shadow of anonymity, to look upon as one of the rarest poets of the century, was born at Bredfield, in Suffolk, on the 31st of March, 1809. He was the third son of John Purcell...   Music Pages 172

Ancient Law *by Henry Maine*   ISBN: *1-59462-128-4* **$29.95**
The chief object of the following pages is to indicate some of the earliest ideas of mankind, as they are reflected in Ancient Law, and to point out the relation of those ideas to modern thought.   Religion/History Pages 452

Far-Away Stories *by William J. Locke*   ISBN: *1-59462-129-2* **$19.45**
"Good wine needs no bush, but a collection of mixed vintages does. And this book is just such a collection. Some of the stories I do not want to remain buried for ever in the museum files of dead magazine-numbers an author's not unpardonable vanity..."   Fiction Pages 272

Life of David Crockett *by David Crockett*   ISBN: *1-59462-250-7* **$27.45**
"Colonel David Crockett was one of the most remarkable men of the times in which he lived. Born in humble life, but gifted with a strong will, an indomitable courage, and unremitting perseverance...   Biographies/New Age Pages 424

Lip-Reading *by Edward Nitchie*   ISBN: *1-59462-206-X* **$25.95**
Edward B. Nitchie, founder of the New York School for the Hard of Hearing, now the Nitchie School of Lip-Reading, Inc, wrote "LIP-READING Principles and Practice". The development and perfecting of this meritorious work on lip-reading was an undertaking...   How-to Pages 400

A Handbook of Suggestive Therapeutics, Applied Hypnotism, Psychic Science   ISBN: *1-59462-214-0* **$24.95**
by Henry Munro   Health/New Age/Health/Self-help Pages 376

A Doll's House: and Two Other Plays *by Henrik Ibsen*   ISBN: *1-59462-112-8* **$19.95**
Henrik Ibsen created this classic when in revolutionary 1848 Rome. Introducing some striking concepts in playwriting for the realist genre, this play has been studied the world over.   Fiction/Classics/Plays 308

The Light of Asia *by sir Edwin Arnold*   ISBN: *1-59462-204-3* **$13.95**
In this poetic masterpiece, Edwin Arnold describes the life and teachings of Buddha. The man who was to become known as Buddha to the world was born as Prince Gautama of India but he rejected the worldly riches and abandoned the reigns of power when...   Religion/History/Biographies Pages 170

The Complete Works of Guy de Maupassant *by Guy de Maupassant*   ISBN: *1-59462-157-8* **$16.95**
"For days and days, nights and nights, I had dreamed of that first kiss which was to consecrate our engagement, and I knew not on what spot I should put my lips..."   Fiction/Classics Pages 240

The Art of Cross-Examination *by Francis L. Wellman*   ISBN: *1-59462-309-0* **$26.95**
Written by a renowned trial lawyer, Wellman imparts his experience and uses case studies to explain how to use psychology to extract desired information through questioning.   How-to/Science/Reference Pages 408

Answered or Unanswered? *by Louisa Vaughan*   ISBN: *1-59462-248-5* **$10.95**
Miracles of Faith in China   Religion Pages 112

The Edinburgh Lectures on Mental Science (1909) *by Thomas*   ISBN: *1-59462-008-3* **$11.95**
This book contains the substance of a course of lectures recently given by the writer in the Queen Street Hall, Edinburgh. Its purpose is to indicate the Natural Principles governing the relation between Mental Action and Material Conditions...   New Age/Psychology Pages 148

Ayesha *by H. Rider Haggard*   ISBN: *1-59462-301-5* **$24.95**
Verily and indeed it is the unexpected that happens! Probably if there was one person upon the earth from whom the Editor of this, and of a certain previous history, did not expect to hear again...   Classics Pages 380

Ayala's Angel *by Anthony Trollope*   ISBN: *1-59462-352-X* **$29.95**
The two girls were both pretty, but Lucy who was twenty-one who supposed to be simple and comparatively unattractive, whereas Ayala was credited, as her Bombwhat romantic name might show, with poetic charm and a taste for romance. Ayala when her father died was nineteen...   Fiction Pages 484

The American Commonwealth *by James Bryce*   ISBN: *1-59462-286-8* **$34.45**
An interpretation of American democratic political theory. It examines political mechanics and society from the perspective of Scotsman James Bryce   Politics Pages 572

Stories of the Pilgrims *by Margaret P. Pumphrey*   ISBN: *1-59462-116-0* **$17.95**
This book explores pilgrims religious oppression in England as well as their escape to Holland and eventual crossing to America on the Mayflower, and their early days in New England...   History Pages 268

www.bookjungle.com *email: sales@bookjungle.com fax: 630-214-0564 mail: Book Jungle PO Box 2226 Champaign, IL 61825*

QTY

The Fasting Cure *by Sinclair Upton*   ISBN: *1-59462-222-1* **$13.95**
In the Cosmopolitan Magazine for May, 1910, and in the Contemporary Review (London) for April, 1910, I published an article dealing with my experiences in fasting. I have written a great many magazine articles, but never one which attracted so much attention... New Age/Self Help/Health Pages 164

Hebrew Astrology *by Sepharial*   ISBN: *1-59462-308-2* **$13.45**
In these days of advanced thinking it is a matter of common observation that we have left many of the old landmarks behind and that we are now pressing forward to greater heights and to a wider horizon than that which represented the mind-content of our progenitors... Astrology Pages 144

Thought Vibration or The Law of Attraction in the Thought World   ISBN: *1-59462-127-6* **$12.95**
by William Walker Atkinson   *Psychology/Religion Pages 144*

Optimism *by Helen Keller*   ISBN: *1-59462-108-X* **$15.95**
Helen Keller was blind, deaf, and mute since 19 months old, yet famously learned how to overcome these handicaps, communicate with the world, and spread her lectures promoting optimism. An inspiring read for everyone... Biographies/Inspirational Pages 84

Sara Crewe *by Frances Burnett*   ISBN: *1-59462-360-0* **$9.45**
In the first place, Miss Minchin lived in London. Her home was a large, dull, tall one, in a large, dull square, where all the houses were alike, and all the sparrows were alike, and where all the door-knockers made the same heavy sound... Childrens/Classic Pages 88

The Autobiography of Benjamin Franklin *by Benjamin Franklin*   ISBN: *1-59462-135-7* **$24.95**
The Autobiography of Benjamin Franklin has probably been more extensively read than any other American historical work, and no other book of its kind has had such ups and downs of fortune. Franklin lived for many years in England, where he was agent... Biographies/History Pages 332

Name	
Email	
Telephone	
Address	
City, State ZIP	

☐ **Credit Card**   ☐ **Check / Money Order**

Credit Card Number	
Expiration Date	
Signature	

Please Mail to: Book Jungle
PO Box 2226
Champaign, IL 61825
or Fax to: 630-214-0564

ORDERING INFORMATION
web*: www.bookjungle.com*
email*: sales@bookjungle.com*
fax*: 630-214-0564*
mail*: Book Jungle PO Box 2226 Champaign, IL 61825*
or PayPal *to sales@bookjungle.com*

Please contact us for bulk discounts

DIRECT-ORDER TERMS

20% Discount if You Order Two or More Books
Free Domestic Shipping!
Accepted: Master Card, Visa,
Discover, American Express